MEMORY IMPROVES QUICKLY

Memory Improvement Techniques to Help You to Have Success in Life

---

By

William Bell

any policies, processes, or directions contained within is the solitary and utter responsibility of the recipient reader. Under no circumstances will any legal responsibility or blame be held against the publisher for any reparation, damages, or monetary loss due to the information herein, either directly or indirectly.

Respective authors own all copyrights not held by the publisher.

The information herein is offered for informational purposes solely and is universal as so. The presentation of the information is without a contract or any type of guarantee assurance.

The trademarks that are used are without any consent, and the publication of the trademark is without permission or backing by the trademark owner. All trademarks and brands within this book are for clarifying purposes only and are owned by the owners themselves, not affiliated with this document.

Table of Contents

INTRODUCTION

There exist a sinking sensation; when you realize something important is missing and can't think what it might be, it is an unpleasant experience.

Then you come back home, and you are greeted by a Happy New Year!'" Or have forgotten you have to be somewhere else–a school function for your son, a report to be delivered, a customer to meet, etc.

You know it has to stop with the absence of another important event with parents, work or friends. It is time to improve your memory before you destroy your future and personal life. There are several learning strategies that any average person can do to improve memory skills greatly.

You can break into groups the things you need to recall. For each class, you will need slightly different memory improvement methods. Dates and activities, faces and names, details, and lists are available.

Forgetting names and faces is one of the most common problems for many people. Many may use situational imaging to identify names and faces, such as associating names with features that stand out.

There are things you can do to improve your memory by remembering a long series of numbers such as the telephone number, the social security number, and a PIN.

Improving your memory is a continuous process, and so do it regularly. In this GUIDE, you will learn how to manage and store information more efficiently with these strategies of memory improvement, retain them, and develop your life and memorization skills.

Happy reading

CHAPTER 1

Memory Improvement Concepts

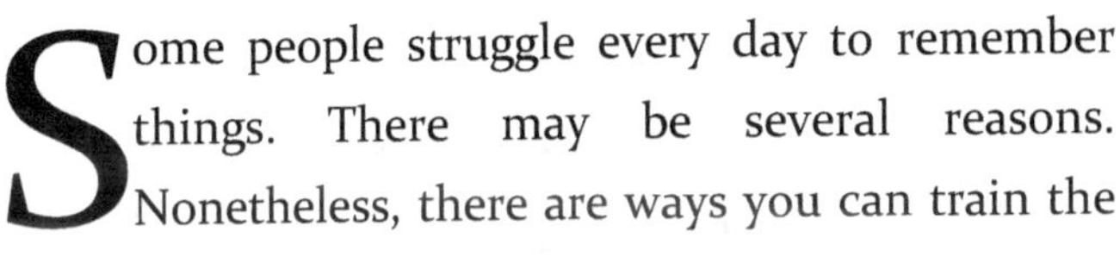

Some people struggle every day to remember things. There may be several reasons. Nonetheless, there are ways you can train the brain to improve memory.

Certain factors are responsible for each side of your brain. For example, on the left side of your brain, numbers, terms, logic, sequence, interpretation, and other elements are taught.

Light, form, creativity, rhythm, and the big picture dwells on the right side of your brain. Both parts come to life on both sides of the brain. Other techniques can be used to improve memory.

Better memory can help link objects with no connection of any kind. It can help you keep things in the right order. You can use some of the other approaches to get your brain where it should be.

You can learn to tell different stories if you want to tell a story, which you will remember for a long time to come. Stories can send a message and help to create dreams that boost your memory.

The use of numbers is another way to improve memory. You can say the numbers in the right sequence to recover your memory. There is nothing more than the right way to count. Once you get the strategies down, you should note that it's going to be frustrating. You will not forget, however, that the strategies are innate in your brain.

You can recall several names from your office, your neighborhood, and around the street. You can also keep those holidays, conferences, and other planned events in mind. It is awe-inspiring to remember the weeks and months ahead.

For strategies for memory improvement, you don't have to strain and fail to recall one and the other. It can be frustrating and painful to try and struggle to remember things. Only imagine if you have run into someone you haven't seen in a couple of months. You may be disappointed if you can't remember their name.

Today we all understand that a brain is an incredible tool, and it is obvious to brain scientists that we must continue to use it or lose it, so what can we do regularly to keep our brain in top condition?

It's fairly common for us to find that we're pretty sure what we know when we listen or read it. It is essential, and we understand what is happening. But within quite a short time, we found that specifics had faded out of our short memories, and it is quite hard to recall the meaning of our new learning.

The question is that we didn't "file" the details when we got it. We only behaved like a sponge, but the sponge again dropped details. What we had to do was to be much more involved in processing the information as it was obtained.

You should, for example, have a sheet of paper and several colored pencils to make notes and diagrams while you listen, if you are learning something new.

You will begin to label the information you accumulate with different colors; in other words, you allocate it to different mental files. You can make notes in one color about aspects of the new content that you can easily connect to your existing information.

For any information related to the context and concepts behind the new information, another color could be used.The color is noted for its main characteristics or features. By listening to or reading a guidebook about a speaker, the new information is structured.

It will be much simpler to track and archive because your notes were checked. That's a way to keep the memory circuits running and the information back in long-term storage!) Because it's already divided into logical pieces.

Even if you don't write creatively-which can be challenging if you are at a lecture and not at a desk, you can use this technique to learn something new.

It helps a lot to arrange it in your brain. You can add it to things you already understand and care about, which makes it so much easier to remember.

The more you associate a set of new information or ideas with what you already know, the more connections you need to find when you need to learn. You will sit there in your subconscious before you enter your conscious mind.

There is no way that is right for everybody. Each person has his strengths and preferred methods to get a brain in shape. Take some time to do your best work and then have fun.

The more enjoyable you find doing these activities, the better because the level of a nice hormone called dopamine is available in your body, and you will find that with this help if you think more creatively. It's a win-win situation; you're feeling good and learning well. What could be better?

CHAPTER 2

Memory Improvement Concentration and Effect

As the title suggests, focus influences the development of memory. You can improve your memory by increasing your focus. Concentration is the secret here now.

To achieve full concentration, you have to focus on what you do and think about. Concentration helps memorization, and concentration will have helped you do so easier if you need to try and remember any particular information.

The great news for you is that concentration is a mental ability you can develop yourself. There are two ways in which you can boost concentration:

First, regardless of your situation, you can try to step up the level of focus that your brain can achieve. Put it differently, try to pay more attention than normal.

Second, create an environment that will allow you to focus much more easily. The formation of an appropriate environment is very critical when you take part in an activity that requires full attention. For instance: try to memorize a poem.

Brain Energy

The development in focus will take a little time and effort, but it can be worth doing. Most people notice a difference in their ability to focus in just a short time.

Several books addressing the subject of neuro-plasticity indicate that the structure and function of the adult brain do not fall into stone as scientists have always believed.

On the opposite, when you learn something new, like a talent, learn new knowledge by heart or improve the way you do things, the brain's connections and neurons will change and develop.

This finding itself is quite remarkable because it offers more evidence that your brain's capacity to concentrate in a way that is already successful can still be further improved. Such improvements do not take effect on the spot according to studies. For change to begin to show, you should continue to work on it daily because what you are doing changes your mind.

You probably have a question now, how can I start improving my concentration?

What Are the Most Effective Ways?

One answer is to try to fit into new habits that increase the power of your mind. Some of these habits include games that boost your attention. Research shows that the more these abilities are used, the greater their brain presence. Therefore, playing games based on concentration and games can improve the ability of your concentration.

Adopt a healthier way to choose the foods you consume: the correct nutrients should be given to your brain to concentrate properly. It requires proper blood sugar control since insulin is the essential nutrient the brain absorbs.

Meditation:

Try meditating twice a day, about 5 minutes a day before going to sleep.

Sleep and Rest:

Sleep and rest are important, as you won't concentrate on the activities of your next day without having plenty of them, possibly leading to poor results on your behalf.

Build the ideal environment: besides adapting the behaviors as mentioned earlier to your daily schedule, build an area that allows you to better focus on an activity that requires your attention.

Improve your motivation by recompensing you. If your work is not exactly fun, but something you only do because it needs to be done, then you can build a bonus for yourself that will make you more inspired as you carry on your job. For example, when your favorite comedy starts within an hour, you have to do your job so you can watch the sitcom in an hour.

When you think of the motivational occurrence in an hour, it can help motivate you further and make you feel better when you finish your work.

Stop Upsetting Yourself.

Avoid any loud sounds that may disturb you and change your position if it is not possible. You may want to learn that playing gentle music of instrumental nature can have a positive impact on your focus.

The human brain is well known to be routine. Specialize in your setting to sustain your concentration-intensive tasks. Try to maintain the quality of the same types of activities each time in the same location.

Stop doing tasks like your hobbies where your mind and body are used to other things. For example, if your family gathers in your living room to watch TV, you may lose concentration.

The Role of Memory Colors:

It may sound odd or weird, but the human brains are affected by colors according to a study. Greenlight increases focus, so buy green bulbs and place them where it's dark, and if the green light doesn't work, then get orange!

Yes, that's right! Since another study shows that red does not only increase focus but also memory, green color likewise stimulates the imagination!

CHAPTER 3

What You Should Know
to Achieve Memory Improvement

emory loss is normal. It usually happens when we age. But if you don't keep your brain healthy and active, memory loss will happen sooner. The good news is the fact that you can now boost your memory.

Today you can choose to boost your memory. Most of us have a good memory, but we don't use it effectively. There can be some issues with a faulty memory, and mental conditions may also arise. But the question now is, "How can you boost your memory?"

Did you notice that recalling stuff in high school or college was much easier than it is now? This is because the brain is not correctly primed to understand.

You studied, read books, did homework, took tests, and took part in a lot of school activities when you were still in class. You have been very busy with your brain. Like everyone who tries to stay fit and healthy, the brain must be worked out so that it is preserved and a good memory created.

You should relax and meditate. It will be hard for you to recall if you're uptight. Therefore, once you know, you have to relax, do it completely. It will only get worse when we think about missing something. Just try and relax. The more relaxed you are, the more information you can recall, process, and absorb. You must be comfortable, mentally, and physically.

Get More Rest. Get More Sleep.

Enough sleep will help remind you of the past. It also helps you reinforce what you learned that day. That's why you have a lot of rest. Rapid eye movement and REM sleep is asleep, which is very helpful in improving memory.

The more likely you are to sleep, the more likely you are to have a lot of REM sleep. Therefore, sleeping is good for your overall health. It's also one of the best ways to improve your memory.

Practice What You've Gotten.

You can transfer information from short-term to long-term memory by repeating what you have learned over and over again. It'll be easier for you to forget when that knowledge is in your long-term memory.

Do not forget to eat healthy foods. It is essential to eat fruits and vegetables. Avoid oily foods. The mind still works, even when you sleep, 24 hours a day. That's why it's crucial not to miss the meat. If your belly is empty, concentration and attention will be more difficult for you.

There are many reasons why you can start losing your memory. This could be because you have had a stressful time, and you don't focus on things entirely and more consistently. It might also be that you've grown up, and your mind is not as vivid as it used to be.

Regardless of the reason for your memory loss, there are many things you can do to boost your memory. Let's take a look at some stuff you might consider.

First of all, you should take some vitamin supplements. In general, vitamin supplements B6 and

B12 are designed to improve the functioning of the brain in terms of information processing and better memory performance. You can choose to take a multivitamin if you take these supplements to achieve the best results.

You must also workout. Evidence has shown that if you can exercise at least 30 to 60 minutes every day, you can increase the benefits of your brain functions and boost your memory.

We also feel that training is just something that can make you fit and healthy to look as good as possible. Nevertheless, most memory benefits are also correlated with a lot of exercises. One of these is helping to improve your memory, so you should try and improve your exercise levels if you consider yourself a little more forgetful.

It is also a good idea to use the body to stimulate your brain. To do that, you can try playing through memory games. Most shops sell these kinds of games, and this should help stimulate the brain.

It is also very important to eat the right kind of meat. Boots with a high content of vitamin C can help to improve your memory. You must ensure that every day, you get the correct supply of the fruit that is rich in this vitamin. Blueberries and oranges are good examples.

Your lifestyle will also play a major role. If you are a drinker, you will probably see that your memory is getting worse and worse. In contrast to this stress, memory loss is also a very important factor. If you are very depressed and you lead a busy life, you must try to adopt some relaxation techniques that will help you feel overwhelmed and boost your memory.

It is possible to improve memory. Learn to use these simple tips to strengthen your memory and to integrate them into your everyday routine, and you will see a major improvement in your memory and life.

CHAPTER 4

Top Memory Improvement Myths

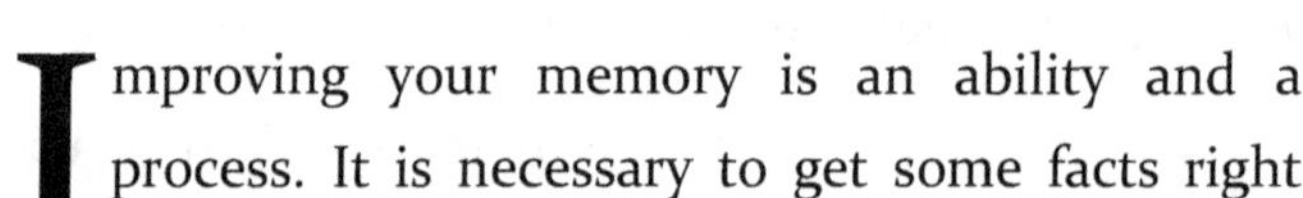

Improving your memory is an ability and a process. It is necessary to get some facts right about your brain before you start this phase. Nothing is sadder than the fact that we can't function by believing in certain memory theories. How are you going to come out of this?

Memory recovery has several theories. I will discuss the top three myths. I know that these are the most common theories because the questions that people ask most often include these topics in training programs.

MYTH 1: The best way for memory improvement is to take memory pills and tonics.

Fact: Most pills and tonics works but in a very limited way. Such drugs are certainly good for your brain's well-being. Such drugs are good for your "healthy brain."

Please realize that a healthy brain does not equal sharper brains automatically. And if your brain is safe, you're not sure if you'll have a huge memory.

To clarify this idea, I'll give you a good analogy. Some medicines/pills etc. may be taken to have strong and healthy hands. Does that mean that you can play the piano? If you want to play the piano, you should train your hands to do this. It requires patience and commitment. It's not enough to have good feet.

Likewise, it won't be enough to have a "healthy brain," although it helps. You need to train your brain for that if you want a great memory. Memory improvement strategies are the best way to improve your memory. Such techniques give your brain really good training and develop your "memory muscles."

MYTH 2: Once I reach the age of 40, my cognitive capacity will deteriorate.

Fact: Age is never a dissuasive source of education. Yet memorizing is a skill. Everyone can learn any ability at any age. What is required of you is the "will to try." Have you not heard of people taking ballroom classes at the age of 50? And you must have seen a lot of 60-year-olds jogging on the roads every night.

Now they have chosen the prospect of learning new skills. If a person can choose to be fit physically at 60, nothing can prevent him from being mentally fit. The keyword here is "ACTION." You can boost your memory regardless of your age if you are willing to act.

MYTH 3: I'm doing myself a disservice by using more of my mind because I use the precious space in my brain.

Fact: Possibly, the "greatest" myth. Your brain has more than a million computers in storage capacity. You can never use the brain's full potential in your life. It's unlikely.

What you ought to learn here is an awesome lesson for your brain: "The more you remember, the more you can think." The more you bring your brain to exercise, the better it gets.

Through hooking it to the existing information in your mind, you are learning new knowledge. The more you know, the more hooks in your brain you make. The greater the "hooks" in your mind, the more you can "stick" to your brain.

CHAPTER 5

Memory Improvement Stumbling Blocks

Do you have a good memory?

Can you remember any information faster?

Whenever you want, can you remember the information?

If your answer to the questions is "No" or "Often," you should know the three memory improvement stumbling blocks. The knowledge of these frames would also be of great help to you. So what are these stumbling blocks?

1. Skepticism

Many people have a "superb degree" of skepticism that they don't even bother to memorize new information.

When I write a 50-digit number and ask anyone to memorize it, I often get some good answers like:

"You mean the whole 50-digit number?

Memorize what?

"I'm going to take one year," and so on.

But what's interesting to note is that no one wants to do it, what triggers people's memory unbelief?

The simple answer is "a lack of awareness." Your mind is the most incredible machine on the planet. When you train your brain, nothing is impossible.

Remember this: You have to ensure that the information is not interesting enough.

2. Disuse

The fastest way to lose knowledge is not to use it in your daily life. Research shows that people forget about 80% of new information in less than 24 hours. Incredible, isn't it? You use the information you learn to stop the lack of knowledge to the greatest extent possible.

Several thoughts are
1. Teach someone else the details.
2. Speak to your colleagues about the points.
3. Write a review in your own words.
4. Write about a chapter!
5. Consider how you can teach a five-year-old child.

Any change in memory is possible if you study these three stumbling blocks. The removal of these blocks early in the processing cycle can save you a lot of time and mental energy. You are the first step to improving memory from the pits of doubt, disinterest, and disuse. It's easy if you take action.

CHAPTER 6

Why Brain Training Is So Important

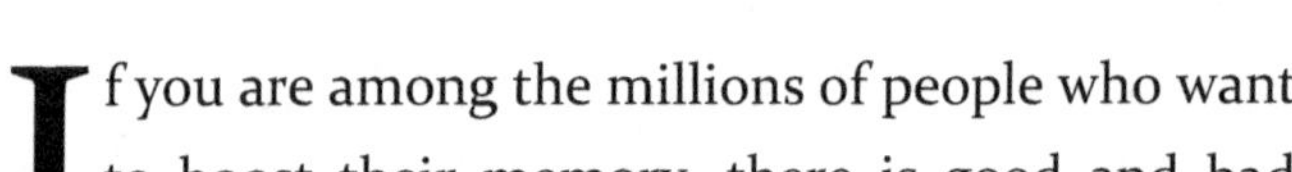

If you are among the millions of people who want to boost their memory, there is good and bad news in the old saying.

The good news first. There are hundreds of players, courses, and audio tapes for memory improvement.

But the Bad News Is Here...

Almost every CD, ebook, or audiotape teaches you the theory but doesn't teach you how to apply the theory consistently.

Let's Use a Handy Example.

You wanted to be a great guitar player, say. You could read a guitar magazine or go to an Eric Clapton concert. But what a great guitar player needs is to practice a certain number of specified qualifications and make them a part of his daily life.

You have to understand how it works first to develop your memory. It is not part of your brain; it is the outcome of many variables. Memory has a functional attentive capacity. It's also about visualizing, like knowing where to turn as you drive. So memory skills need to be able to think quickly, including remembering the name of a person.

And since the quality of memory is measured by several brain functions, increasing the overall brain function makes perfect sense.

How Can Your Brain Be Educated?

Your brain is powerful, as you might expect. It has immense strength, but like a muscle, it won't work if it isn't tested.

You should first analyze how you can learn to train your brain. Through involving all five senses, people learn. Think about it. You learned to see, hear, touch, smell, and taste at some point in your life. That's not just what you know, but how you remember it, too.

In having all your senses active in the learning process, you activate the entire brain. Mostly, you owe it a workout, and it works better. You can see where we go here. A good memory is the result of highly engaged brain capacities.

Your brain can be equipped with strategies that include all senses at some level. It's not about saving a card deck for starters. These methods deal more with the brain's intensive and rigorous training to work as a whole. The only way to do that is through training.

Training your mind to use its full potential is the best technique to improve your memory because all the senses are responsible for your memory. For example, using your hearing sense by listening to a memory tutorial CD is not sufficient.

Mostly, there are hundreds of strategies for improving memory on the market. Be vigilant about anyone who only asks you to use one of your senses and expect results.

CHAPTER 7

How Can You Improve Your Memory!

You will likely find these days that there are more and more things to remember. As a result, you need a good memory. Not everyone has an excellent memory. Most people tend from time to time to forget one thing or the other. If this is the case for you, don't worry, because there are several ways to improve your memory.

The best way to achieve this is to integrate all available methods. In so doing, you will find that you have a better chance of improving your performance. The higher the degree of progress you get, the more likely your memory will be.

There are several benefits to memory improvement. One of these benefits is that you can save the names of the people you have just met. It can be an excellent experience, especially for people who work with many customers.

If you have developed your memory to this level, you have a better chance to deliver exceptional service to your customers, which leads to frequent customers.

It will boost the company's efficiency. The second significant benefit of improving memory is that substantial numbers can be stored in your brain.

It would be helpful to have a bank account number, credit card numbers, telephone number for your next child, etc. in your head for everyday use. This is because if anything unexpected happens, it will be very convenient.

An example of an unexpected event is an incident. In this scenario, you should send your rescuers the telephone numbers for your next child to be aware of your distress.

If you are a public speaker, you will benefit greatly from improving your memory. This improvement can help you memorize speeches in a short time regardless of their duration-so you can make an unexpected appeal!

Many public speakers read and respond to speeches held in front of them because they need improved memory. A public speaker who reads from a speech given to him requires strategies for improving their memory. Those who listen have a good memory too.

In addition to these benefits, others are correlated with improving memory. You can remember events in the news or other media vividly. This means you can quote chapters from newspapers and help with the subject in a discussion.

The average person searches for strategies for memory improvement. Current trends and events in life allow you to be conscious of changes in your memory because you have to recall several things. Perhaps you may be among people who don't have an excellent memory and probably forget something or the other in your everyday routine.

If this is the case, you also need to boost your memory. This is not a very troubling issue, and memory improvement techniques will help. Many of these strategies will help you gain better memory.

It is always best to look around and learn about strategies to boost your memory and merge them to make use of them. This can allow you to achieve a memory level that can be very helpful. Improving memory will help you improve the chances of using improved memory.

Increased memory could offer many advantages. You can then easily remember the names of the people you regularly encounter in your daily social contact. This is particularly useful when you meet other people during your daily work.

This will allow you to impress people, and if they are customers, they will be happy enough to come again and again to you.

You will enable you to be more successful in your job when you work for a company. Such an increase in memory would also help you to recall a number, which is nowadays a significant part of a daily routine.

Telephone numbers are to be recorded, such as bank account numbers, credit card numbers, etc. If of an emergency, knowing your nearest and dearest phone numbers can be a big advantage.

In the case of an accident, recalling your family's telephone number, contact numbers, or medical practitioner will make it easier for your memory to detect the cause of your injuries.

An improved memory as a speaker in the public domain will help you become a speaker who talks more efficiently instead of referring to written notes.

It can be very surprising if you are called to speak without providing having any experience.

Public speakers will generally have pulpits in front of them to hold their speeches primed. You could do with a memory-improving approach that would allow them to communicate more efficiently and to recall points from the notes that they made for the occasion.

Other Benefits of Improved Memory.

You can recall every detailed account of current events that you read or saw on the electronic media. So if the same subjects emerge in a discussion, you can easily give your point of view and also hold people around you.

CHAPTER 8

What Are the Memory Improvement Foods to Eat?

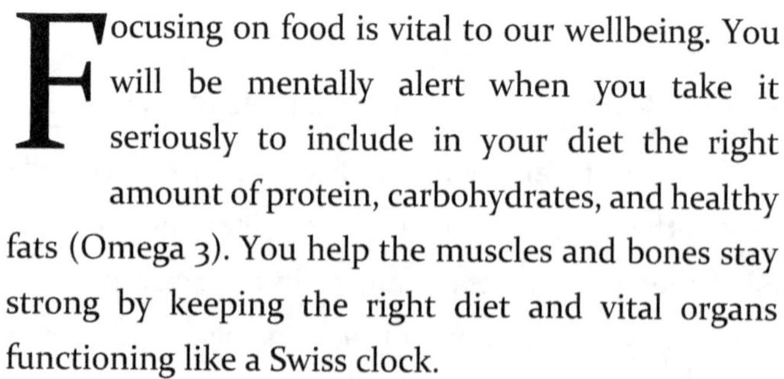

Focusing on food is vital to our wellbeing. You will be mentally alert when you take it seriously to include in your diet the right amount of protein, carbohydrates, and healthy fats (Omega 3). You help the muscles and bones stay strong by keeping the right diet and vital organs functioning like a Swiss clock.

Our brain is no different; you have to supply it with the right nutrients if it is to function properly. A diet rich in the right nutrients will help you jog your memory, remove brain fog, and make your brain work like 10-15 years ago. It makes sense that the brain, as the most important part of our bodies, needs the best nutrients to function correctly.

In the last few years, several extensive studies have shown that some vitamins and minerals are correlated with the proper functioning of the brain. Sugar, for example, gives a brief fast stimulant but disappears quickly after (an hour or two). However, if the sugar rush disappears, we also feel tired and sluggish.

The brain works the same; you would not get a lot of miles from it if you feed it only with candy bars and will also often encounter crashes.

If you want to boost your memory, eating right is very important. Rich foods with antioxidants have proven beneficial for improvement in memory and are long hailed as the number one cancer fighter in our bodies...

In addition to these two essential functions, we now know that they are also necessary for your long-term memory, and it would be prudent for you to ensure that they are integrated into every meal.

Carrots and nuts are only a few antioxidant products; you can also take supplements. Green tea is a reliable source of antioxidants and is very good for your overall body health.

Soy is another experience that brings little gifts to nature. Eating Tofu can help improve your memory and brain function, or you can always drink soy milk if you don't like Tofu.

You can drink soy milk as regular milk, and add it to your tastes, use your imagination, make milkshakes, make chocolate soy milk whatever you like. Soy milk can also be easily purchased; you can find it everywhere.

Most of us prepare our meals with some cooking oil or fat. Okay, why not use the one you can boost your memory?

Olive oil is the number one option, and it would help your brain immensely if you include it in your regular diet. Use it for salad dressing or daily cooking, but don't expose it to light if you don't use it, try to store it in the cool and dark place.

Always consider advertising at the start of your meal preparation, for instance, when you are already washing them and putting them in a tub, or use a frying casserole for cooking meat and advertising a little olive oil when it is done.

If possible, try finding an olive oil produced in Croatia. Croatian olive oil is an exceptional quality, processed in the ancient, organic, non-industrial manner.

You will help the brain and body by changing your diet to improve memory. There's no need for a big change, just good replacements for bad foods are needed, and that's it.

The food you consume not only provides the body with nutrients to maintain its health but also affects the activity of your brain. When you assume that you have a poor memory, you can consider changing your diet plan.

There are many things you can even find in your kitchen to boost your memory.

The examples below are...

Simple memory improvement foods:

- **Fish**- Eating fish is said to be a natural way to improve memory. Omega 3 fatty acids that help improve memory are abundant in fish such as tuna, mackerel, salmon, and sardines. Fish is also a source of DHA, a major component of fatty acid in the brain, and therefore maintains its protection.
- **Berry** –strawberries, cranberries, raspberries, blueberries, and blackberries are abundant in antioxidants that keep memory and coordination functions intact. Studies indicate that drinking berries help block dying brain cells.

- Honey-the natural sweetener and antioxidants is a great source of calcium, iron, and vitamin C. Such antioxidants help remove free radicals from our bodies, prevent cell loss and damage, alleviate fear and improve your memory.
- **Nuts and Seeds**–almonds, walnuts, pumpkin seeds, flax seeds, and others contain vitamin E and omega-3 fatty acids, which are memory-friendly. You can sprinkle nuts on salad or cereal bowl or snack them.
- **Eggs**— Choline-rich eggs are the key chemical requirement for optimum brain health and function. Choline deficiency leads to Alzheimer's initiation. Some other choline-containing products are liver, sardines, peanuts, and soybeans.
- **Green Vegetables** –spinach, Brussels sprouts, cauliflower, kale, and broccoli are some healthy antioxidant sources, which counter free body radicals. Green vegetables are recommended for memory recovery in your diet.

The foods mentioned above are few that can contribute to your memory. And besides the diet, other things can greatly improve the health of the brains. You should also include a regular visit to your doctor.

CHAPTER 9

Sleep and Memory Improvement

Numerous studies to determine the sleep and memory relationship have been carried out. Many findings indicate that the brain can remember better things or concepts, especially when people are to fall into a deep sleep at night.

Although most people believe that their brains work when they sleep, they are most active, particularly when they reach their depths. At this time, the brain starts to interact and organizes all the information that has been processed during active hours.

Research performed to see connections between sleep and memory improvement showed almost the same results in whatever sort of memory research needs to be done.

Such memory tasks involve gathering fact-based information, remembering events or incidents in life, and the patterns followed by a particular procedure.

The subjects involved in the studies in any form of memory work showed positive results, in particular when they slept after their research or reading.

Although most people recall information they learned while they are awake, when they sleep properly, they have a better chance of long-term memory. Research is also carried out to assess the brain's ability to absorb and retain information when it is already tired.

The findings show that the brains of the subjects are harder to learn and consume some information. Sleep deprivation also helps people with negative emotions, often associated with the forgetfulness of important information.

Those who want to develop their memory need to learn how sleep deprivation can affect their brain functions. If they wake and sleep at the natural rhythm of the body and the brain, they are more likely to improve their memory.

While individuals want to carry out overtime in their heads, they should agree that this isn't a good idea as they're just wasting time and will not remember the important things later.

A while ago, some research suggested that sleeping smells can aid learning by improving the brain's ability to retain new memories. New research from Northwestern University has now shown that sound can activate the sleeping brain in much the same way, contributing to the growing evidence that the memories are best stored with optimal sleep.

A study published in the science issue of November 20, 2009, which explores how sound evidence associated with knowledge newly acquired helps the brain hold onto this information.

"We realized that the memory system is quite involved in sleep, and the memory can be reinforced nowadays," said John Rudoy, the study's lead author and Northwestern Ph.D. candidate in neuroscience.

The study's participants, 12 young adults who were asked to learn a new activity and take a nap, were able to maintain their newly learned memory better when they were exposed to sound stimuli during a nap.

The challenge involved showing 50 pictures, each one shown on a computer screen at a time. The photos had a similar sound-a meow with a cat photo, a glass that shattered when seeing a glass of wine.

The job of the subjects was to position the objects in their original location, together with the accompanying tone, sometime later. This part of the study concluded when subjects were able to perform this recall task with all the objects two times.

In the hour after the memory task was done, the subjects had to have a nap in a dark, quiet place. To control brain activity, electrodes have been mounted on their eyes.

The scientists played half the 50 sound signals heard during the training part of the experiment only after checking the subjects were in a deep sleep. Twenty-five new sounds have also been added to the mix.

When they woke up, the topics had the memory function again to do. After a nap, scores were worse than before napping. Researchers believe that memory loss over time is apparent.

But the confirmation that certain pictures were correctly identified after exposing them to sound signals during sleep is far better, even though there was no ability to hear such sounds.

"The study strongly suggests that we don't close our minds during deep sleep," ResearcherRudoy adds,

"Instead, this is an important time to consolidate memories."

So does that mean that there is a way to help us to boost our learning capability?

It's too early to know. Scientists are generally of the belief that existing memories can be improved during sleep, but there is no new information.

The brain plays back memories during sleep, and sounds can activate more specific memories. It requires future work to assess the amount of retention of memory associated with sleep sounds in contrast with more traditional ways of learning...

Like learning and studying, this would allow students and actors all over the world to know who will be more successful, to listen while you sleep, or to practice a little more when you are awake.

People usually need enough sleep to keep their bodies safe. If your body is good, your brains always work very well. All of these help to improve brain power to remember important things or events. Learning the connection between sleep and memory improvement is very helpful in achieving life goals.

CHAPTER 10

How to Use Isochronic Tones to Boost Your Memory

You know what nuisance it is when you can't remember that person's name or where you drop your keys. And the more you strive to recall these things, the more it disappears from memory!

These memory problems are common among people everywhere, and all sorts of methods and strategies are introduced to improve memory-with mixed results.

There is, however, a method that works differently and is very successful, which are ISOCHRONIC TONES. Read on, and you will find out how memory improvement isochronic sound recordings work.

What are the Isochronic Tones?

Isochronic tones are a type of brainwave learning technology based on sound. Brainwave learning (also known as brainwave synchronization) works by helping the brain produce certain frequencies of a brainwave. This is useful, as various brainwave frequency bands are related to different states of mind and abilities.

When you listen to an isochronic tone recording that leads your brain into the theta frequency band, you will begin to produce brain waves that are mostly 5-8 Hz-they is called theta brainwaves.

This theta is perceived as a trance that is deeply relaxed and associated with various psychic and other mental phenomena and by increased access to the subconscious mind.

Brainwave learning allows exposure to many different mental states without having to spend years meditating.

Isochronic tones are generally considered more intense than other types of brainwave learning (such as binaural beats, monaural beats) because they have sound pulses that are clearly defined and replicated easily. Since each pulse is isolated from the next pulse, the brain can monitor and match the frequency more easily.

So, how can isochronic tones boost your memory?

Most people have problems with their memory because they have mental blocks. There are still memories in their subconscious minds, but they cannot be reached by conscious minds.

Since the memories have not completely disappeared, you must be able to remove the blocks to unlock the memory. This can be achieved by exposure to the subconscious mind.

We noticed earlier that it is easier to contact the unconscious when the brain is in the theta state. You can overcome your conscious blocks and retrieve secret memories of your subconscious by listening to an isochronic sound recording that takes you into the theta state.

It works both for short-term and long-term recollections and is a very effective method for many people in comparison to traditional techniques.

Isochronic recordings are very easy to use for memory improvement. You can get a suitable record (either downloaded from the internet or on a CD), find a quiet, convenient place, and then listen and concentrate.

If you are using isochronic tones (unlike binaural beats), you don't have to use headphones, but I'd recommend them anyway because they help to block out noise. Only ensure that the volume is comfortable.

Most people get instant results the first time an isochronic method is used, but this doesn't always happen, so be ready to listen to the recording periodically to make the most of it.

While brainwave learning encourages getting into a profoundly relaxed state to accessing your unconscious memories, the effort still needs to be made by concentrated attention and your dedication to daily use.

When you want to use the power of an isochronic tone to boost your memory, make sure you use a performance file, such as the' Memory Improver ' songs.

CHAPTER 11

Mnemonic Memory Improving Techniques

The mnemonics system uses techniques such as word associations and rhymes to help people memorize knowledge more quickly.

Are you having trouble memorizing the biological method of animal classification?

You will know Country, Phylum, Race, Order, Family, Genus, and Species with the Mnemonic "King Phillip Came Over For Great Spaghetti."

Today, when reading and learning this type of information, I still use techniques like this. It is a simple technique, and it is certainly always useful, whether you are a student or a businessman trying to remember a list of appointments.

Until information can be preserved as a memory, it has first to be downloaded, processed, and classified and stored in your brain through your senses. This information is used to create our understanding of our complicated physical environs. Such memories can then be retrieved, which are already stored in your permanent memory.

Look at the example below. What are some of the first related words to mind when someone says the word "baby?"

You can think of screaming, bottles, rattles, swaddling, and so on. Acronyms are another mnemonics category.

NYPD, short for the New York Police Department, is the term many people know about. Most acronyms end up being used so often as a term. EPCOT is known to anyone who went to Disney World in Florida, but what does it mean? It's an acronym for the Society Of Tomorrow research model.

One of the cleverest strategies I have learned there that I still use today. I still know that months have 30 days and 31. I always have a question. There is a handy mnemonic to remember: "thirty days have September, March, June, and November." This simple rhyme promotes the recollection of the date rather than the time of remembering in all twelve months. The more imaginative and vivid the mnemonic is, the better the long-term memory is. The more crazy and out of the ordinary, the better the performance you will get.

The mnemonic memorization approach is very successful in recalling complex strings of words and lists. Whether you're trying to remember the number of days a month or a medical school graduate, you're sure to find the mnemonic formation is an extremely effective exercise, no matter how complex it is.

Start doing some first, and once you get a few under your belt, you can see how successful the trick is. Soon you will get much better at creating new mnemonics that, to me, is one of the best techniques you can use to develop your memory.

CHAPTER 12

The Peg Method in Memory Improvement

Memory disorder may be a frightening matter, but it does not necessarily mean that you have a medical condition that leads to your memory loss. Sometimes hectic lives are enough to cause us to struggle in our memory if we try to remember something relatively easy else to remember.

There are different ways to strengthen your memory skills through various methods of memory improvement. Nevertheless, some of the suggested recall strategies are repetitive and easy to put into one's daily life.

For example, take the Peg Process.

The peg method may be useful for using the chunking process for calling back telephone numbers; however, its association with letters and numbers is much to be remembered.

Assuming you have a long list of items that you must recall without notes, if you don't have time to set up associations, you don't use the Peg process.

So how can you improve your memory skills easily?

First off, there are no two people, and everyone has a different learning style. Many people may be visual students, and others may be more hands-on. Others can do better by mastering video.

You must first understand the preferred style to learn strategies for memory improvement. Additionally, you need to understand the ease with which skills are applied.

Do you have time to manage them in your everyday life?

Ultimately, when you know a different combination of learning styles, the learning styles deliver versatile techniques.

For some, the Peg technique can work wonders to improve their memory, but it can fall on deaf ears on others. The best methods for memory improvement will improve all types and senses and anticipate smell and taste if you choose to eat while you are studying.

You can sit and snack using strategies like those learned during Memory Improvement courses while learning useful techniques that improve your memory considerably but promote all sides of your mind to function with every type of learning.

By reading easy to understand books on how to improve your memory, you can immediately improve your memory skills by playing with the program in both games and practical hands-on learning techniques.

A brain is a beautiful and powerful thing than any machine. You will begin to remember things after the skills you learned you did not even know that you had put in that amazing terminal. You don't have to lose much but much to gain in memory, so the Peg Method is used if you want to recall different lists of things.

The most common ones are for school and work. A memory improvement system provides information that needs to be in a certain order. It acts as a filing office for the restoration of information.

The Peg system usually works for 1 to 20 numbers and the whole alphabet. This includes new items together with the old items you are working on. The Peg Method uses a mental component to "hang" the knowledge you want to keep in mind. This part helps to return the information to your memory bank.

This helps you to recall the things you need to know when using the Peg Method for memory improvement. You can get more information and more things. The use of numerical pins helps you to find out how the objects should be identified. So you can say, "Number 3 belongs to this number."

If you have several things in sequence, you can use the Peg method as much as you need.

With this technique for improving your memory, you can store various lists of things simultaneously while using this tool. You can learn to memorize a lot of information when you leave room between these lists and use the pegs with other methods.

You can be versatile using the Peg Process. Many approaches use rhymes with numbers and shapes. The way you use them varies according to the Peg processes. It allows you to minimize interruptions by keeping the information you want and need in your memory bank.

You can also use pegs with other programs like the Loci framework for memory upgrades. If you do that, you will remember a lot of information.

Using an alphabet with the Peg Method, you will remember a lot of details. You need a memory reference in a 10-sequence string. This is related to each alphabet letter.

The Peg system is useful when you deal with a lot of alphabet numbers and letters. You would have a brain filing system you don't want to get rid of. This system can help you to go a long way.

Speed Reading Technique for Memory Improvement

Although memory improvements are possible in a range of ways; speed reading is recognized by people around the world as one of the most successful. Proper reading strategies not only help you double your reading rate but also keep information for a long time and enjoy good concentration and focus.

If you want to try it now, here are some methods to help you master speed reading:

o **Chunking:** break complex information into parts with or less than seven components.

Because your conscious brain can arrange and handle only about seven pieces at a time, chopping information can allow you to learn more easily and remember a lot of information for a long time to come. The use of mnemonics can be an ideal way to achieve this function.

- Skimming: learn how to skim the whole information with keywords and sentences without reading any words on the page. By skipping those parts that have little effect on their overall context, you can process information faster than in the conventional way of reading every word.

  - **Elimination of sub-vocalization:** if you read aloud, the brain's ability to interpret words before they are spoken is more time-consuming than if you read silently. Many research results have shown that, when the first and last alphabet is in place, the mind can recognize the arrangement of the other letters as each part is logically put in place.

Learn to read quietly without pronouncing every word in your head, so that you can read a choice much quicker and retain it in your memory. No wonder this is an effective strategy for improving memory. Although you may be drawn into an active memory restoration strategy, be patient and persistent in your work.

There are no tried and true approaches that function for all. If you want to learn how to read quickly, the best way is, as described above, to practice and study the different methods used by speed readers and pick those that best suit your needs.

While memory improvement techniques are numerous, speed reading is hailed by people around the world as one of the most effective. Fixed speed calculation methods not only help you increase your reading speed, but also keep the information for a long time and improve your concentration and focus.

CHAPTER 14

Free IQ Tests to Track Your Growth in Memory

Many people like to have a better memory and also want to be smarter. In this chapter, I want to talk about how brain development and improvement of memory can be integrated and how you can track your progress using free IQ tests.

There have been methods for memory improvement for such a long time, even thousands of years. The strategy of Memory Palace,' also known as the' locus' approach, is thought to have been used a few hours ago but is still incredibly effective today.

Using these strategies not only benefits your memory, but it also exercises your mind and eventually will increase your brainpower.

It also works; otherwise, brain training strategies will eventually also boost your processing and bring you up to date with any free IQ tests.

To begin training your mind, you can start a few easy strategies immediately:

Solve Sudoku and other logic puzzles every day.

Often take another route to work.

Try to explain to someone something unbelievably complex once in a while.

Such ideas may at first seem basic, but if they are implemented regularly, you can almost immediately see the effects. Set aside 5 minutes a day, and you're going to do well, as long as you keep track of your progress.

Now I've been talking about free IQ tests already a little, but how can they help you?

Search for Google ' free IQ test' or something similar, and you can take a lot of free IQ tests. If you practice your brain training and your improvement in memory, set a time for yourself when you want to check yourself, once a week would be my option.

Each time, it is important to do a different test. Why?

Because you will understand the questions once you have checked, and this usually leads to a highly inflated answer. While you get different results from the different IQ tests you take, you see a trend line developing over time, and your brainpower rises greatly along with your memory.

CHAPTER 15

Memory Improvement Link Method

Poor memory isn't just something for an elderly or aged adult; it can affect anybody regardless of any age. Many strategies help people improve their memory, but not all are as simple as they like to claim.

Others take time, which is partly why people tend to have poor memory, lack of time to pay enough attention to things they need to store in their memory.

A recall is an established technique that takes place from an early age in our brain. If it's over, it can be quite clear.

If like I suggest, you are a lackey daisy about your memory, I have to take a mental note of it and, while your brain may have remembered, they did not give it enough information to recall later, when it was required; When the old memory bank draws this particular information later it will fail.

A technique called the reference method is used to create a great memory. This helps you to remember the stored information because of the way you packed this.

The LINK method uses mnemonics, a relation between two objects or products. It gives the brain instructions to be used for a later reminder of the stored information. This can be achieved in a term or tale connection.

Tell us that you prepare for a lesson, any exam and that you must recall all of the bones in your foot. Next, you'd write a list of all bones in your foot.

Since writing the description of what looks like,

5 metatarsal for each foot,

14 phalanges per foot (3 phalanges per foot, except hallux with only 2),

Talus, Calcaneus, Navicular, Cuboid, Inner cuneiform, Middle cuneiform, and External cuneiform for 26 bones per foot.

First, you should take the words and place them in a story form or in a word association that you can always remember easier. It could be something like five metatarsals= five mega-parcels in one-word association= tomorrow;

I will get five mega parcels (metatarsals) out of 14 philanders= 14 phalanges.

You will proceed in this way with word association until all the appropriate terms were included in the list.

In history, you tell a story with a combination of word association and a narrative. There might be something like this:

Five little metatarsals took off when the terrifying fanged phalanges leaped out of the blue 14 out of the bush.

Except for the little one, Hallux, who had only two, each had three fangs. Again, you would do the same until you used all of the terms mentioned. This is called the LINK Process.

The reference approach is a reliable way of recalling items, even if it depends on the person who remembers the story or the word associations. This tool, however, with a combination of other techniques, allows you to improve your memory dramatically.

CHAPTER 16

Hypnosis and Memory Improvement

Some people may want to explore the idea that hypnosis can specifically improve your memory. Different areas of human efforts have been applied where hypnosis has been used, and the potential to be successful in improving the brain memory functions is good.

Psychologists may have used it on their patients, for instance, to recall such events that their conscious mind cannot recover from.

Often, people don't remember things or information from past times because they have hidden them deep like those who have done so much harm to them. But those who attend therapy should know everything to deal with it.

Many people can sometimes suffer from anxiety, and the situation tends to make them know what they need, such as lessons learned for an exam or the information required for a job interview.

One way people can reduce their pressure is to relax with hypnosis. Individuals can focus better when they are comfortable and can also absorb information easily and recall it in such situations.

There are services today that help people relax through hypnosis. Nevertheless, many people can opt for therapeutic hypnotherapy if they don't know what to do and have many emotional problems. However, people can also attempt to hypnotize themselves at home so that they can improve their ability to remember.

If you find it a little hard to relax, you can try some mental exercises involving all the other parts of your body before you achieve complete relaxation of your body and mind.

These can also include symbolism that will help their minds concentrate until they are in a trance. When people arrive at their evocative state, they can use self-commands to improve their memory capacities. You can also reassure yourself that nothing will stop you from learning everything you have learned.

This method is like manipulating the conscious mind so that the order goes straight to the unconscious state of your brain. Yet people have to think about it positively, and it will work for them.

You should also do so several times before you can achieve the results you are looking for. Those who need help should test programs to get better memory capacity by self-hypnosis.

Hypnosis is one of the best ways to improve memory. This is because the brain records an activity, thinking, or feeling that is preserved in the unconscious until retrieved.

Also, items that might not have seemed significant, your subconscious keeps or stores all you've ever seen. Your unconscious is like a big information base that holds all the knowledge you saw, heard, or thought. Occasionally, when we can't remember anything. Hypnosis comes in.

When you can't remember anything, like something important or memory that seems to be lost, hypnosis can help you reach the place where this information is stored.

Sometimes we don't remember anything because our subconscious has distorted our recollection of it, and sometimes we don't remember something, because we can't focus hard enough to find it.

A trained hypnotist can locate and eliminate any blocks in our subconscious utilizing a variety of hypnosis techniques and substitute the blocks with true statements preventing the subconscious.

Your hypnotist can also reprogram how memory can be processed in the subconscious, such as the removal of a messy filing cabinet or defragmentation of our internal information servers to make your memories more available.

If you have always been crazy in your search for a misplaced object, or if you can't remember the name of the person you met earlier in the day, it's very frustrating.

One of the best ways to improve information storage is to maintain a consistent retrieval process. Using hypnosis, the hypnotist will place you in hypnotic positions that relax your brain, remove obstacles, and increase your concentration on some unconscious areas. It helps you to restore your particular memory.

For example, maybe you would never discover the combination code of your new wall safely. Yet you forget, in time, where this hiding place is. Your hypnotizer will relax your mind and help your subconscious concentrate on the day you hide your mix.

When you ask a series of questions related to that specific day and period, you will recall where the combination is while your mind is in a highly focused state. Hypnosis helps you find lost objects, or recover forgotten memories, and improves the process of storage and retrieval.

We may not recall important things like holidays or anniversaries, because our unconscious associated them with a distressing or disturbing occurrence from your history. In this situation, we cannot recall what we lost, no matter how hard we try.

The Hypnos will eliminate any obstacles in the recovery process by helping the mind to understand that the pain or anger of the past has no place in today's events. It helps the subconscious to distinguish it from what you are trying to remember. If your subconscious is triggered by hypnosis, it will boost your memory.

Many people gasp as the word ' hypnosis' is used. We apply to a scenario in which a hypnotist makes people, who are taken from a show crowd, do all sorts of stupid things like clucking and stumbling like a chicken. Many people are afraid that they will be under another person's control and are therefore hesitant to be hypnotized.

Nevertheless, you can control your hypnosis and support yourself in so many ways by self-hypnosis. For example, self-hypnosis can help you stop smoking, stop binge eating, manage depressive outbreaks, and also help improve your memory.

Memory improvements can be accomplished by self-hypnosis by breaking down the mental blockages that stop you from remembering things sufficiently. The art of self-hypnosis must first be learned. And once you are capable of self-hypnosis, you can monitor and correct a wide range of problem areas (including your memory capacities).

Different DVDs, videos, and audiotapes can be purchased that will direct you through the self-hypnosis process. We differ in content but usually teach you step-by-step how to relax, which is one of the keys of self-hypnosis. You can then channel your subconscious to boost your memory when you are in a relaxed state.

To start the process of improving memory through self-hypnosis, you first need to close your eyes and fully relax your body.

You should breathe deeply and methodically before the heart slows down. If you have trouble relaxing, why not imagine manipulating every part of your body. Every part of your body, you say to relax from your toes to your neck. If you think you are in a relaxed state, count down from 20 to zero.

It helps to imagine you sit at the top of the staircase and walk down the staircase every time you count. When you get to zero and reach the bottom of the escalator, you have to be strong enough to start to work on improving your memory through self-hypnosis.

You will start to improve your memory by self-hypnosis once you are relaxed and hypnotic. All you have to do is say that you want your memory to improve. You tell your mind that whenever you hear or read something, you can find this information when you need it.

You can also reassure yourself that all the blockages you experience should disappear so that you do not remember things. This is a great way to improve your memory, and it works well.

You talk to your subconscious as you engage in self-hypnosis, and you start to talk to yourself. This is how hypnotizers can get you to do things you wouldn't normally because they can manipulate your subconscious mind.

To make self-hypnosis the most effective, you really must believe that self-hypnosis can be used positively and helpfully and believe that it works. This belief and recognition are the most important steps in this whole process.

Once you have learned and consistently practiced the art of self-hypnosis, you will start to remember more than you have ever thought. So why not sit back, close your eyes, breathe rhythmically, and begin your journey through your hypnosis now.

CHAPTER 17

Memory Improvement with the Clustering Method

A good memory is an important quality for you to succeed in today's fast-moving, informative society. It is crucial to your success to remember important details such as names, images, figures, dates, events, and other components of everyday life.

You don't need to worry about forgetting or losing important items when you have a good memory, and you can overcome mental barriers to prevent reaching your full job, home, and love capacity.

Your memory is regulated by a complex brain network of interconnected neurons that can store millions of information independently. It is this capacity of your mind to store comprehensive and structured memories of past experiences that allow you to learn and to develop.

Such memory-saved interactions allow you to learn from mistakes, shield yourself from danger, and achieve the goals you set. By using your mind power, you are better able to learn the lessons of life that allow you to avoid future errors based on your own experience and others ' failures.

Poor memory may be the product of a mental disorder or inability to concentrate, disability, lack of attention or poor listening skills, and other bad habits. Luckily you can retrain yourself to improve and fine-tune your memory. The **"CLUSTERING"** method is the typical tool for developing a better memory.

Clustering examples include

1. Numbers, letters, features, and classes are grouped.

2. Grouping similar and opposite words and concepts

3. Grouping of mental images or subjective structure The clustering of information improves memory by splitting information into easier treated bits.

Consider, for example, a 10-digit telephone number with area code. You can easily access this information from your memory bank by saving numbers in groups of three or four.

Clustering words or idea means arranging terms in our minds to help us better remember. It uses the power of connection to remind you of one idea or suggestion. The word pair clusters are one example. These may be synonyms, antonyms, or names. For example, "Fair" and "square," "man" and "girl."

Subjective organization clustering uses information collection classes, procedures, tools, and associations. For example, words are often remembered in groups, depending on the context.

I will address that. Remembering one word triggers recollection of an unrelated word it was grouped or connected with somehow.

Let's take another example of cooking. Each of these individual ingredients has no meaning alone, while there are a variety of ingredients in a recipe. The whole meaning takes shape only through the process of mixing each of these ingredients.

For short, use the following methods to preserve your memory:

1. Think about the problem solving and contextualizing process rather than attempting to memorize information from context.

2. Understand what techniques work best for you. Will you work best with clusters of categories? Or are you more driven visually?

3. Analyze situational facts and experiences to recall significant information and eliminate unnecessary information,

Memory Improvement Based Finding the Best Learning Style

Our memory is so important because it allows us to keep this life in mind for years to come. Of course, when you recall a 15-year-old memory but forget about the food list, that might be so annoying. Most people want to find a way to improve their memory.

Well, in truth, you can do stuff other than deal with disappointment over things you forget.

It is important to examine how things are learned before we engage in memory improvement methods. If you are interested in a new experience and you hear something different, the brain must absorb and decipher this information.

It takes and interprets the information in some respects. Once you concentrate on and learn something new, the brain gathers and stores the information.

It's much like putting information in a filing office you're opening. If you want that knowledge to be recalled again, the brain takes it for you. It is like going back to the filing cabinet and finding the folder you've already marked.

You can recall more than possibly when your memory was good, and you were certainly used to it. When we don't work to keep our brain healthy and to learn new ways that we can think, our ability to remember can start to slip a little.

Consider a Dancer.

While she can spend time practicing for all her movements, she cannot get out and start performing if she stops training if she hasn't worked for many years. So it's also with the brain.

One way to improve your memory is always to be mindful of everything that's happening around you. Most people listen only half when others speak to them. It's easy to focus on something else rather than what you think. Make sure you reflect on what is happening around you so that you can save it and bring it back into the future.

When you get new information, work to connect it to something you already know to make remembering easier. There are several different methods for reading, so figure out what works for you.

Many people remember better when they have visual aids to support. Many learn best by listening to stuff. You can rely on your style of training to further develop your memory.

If you don't know anything, find out more by looking at it yourself. While it may seem hard to understand, it can make more sense for you if you find a different way of learning or another interpretation. Researching on something different let you gain more insight and makes you find out what stuff you need to worry about.

If you want to remember something, think about it and throw it in your brain a few times. The more you repeat in your head, the more you can understand it and remember it in the future.

CHAPTER 19

Memory Improvement by Keeping a Happy Mind

Memory improvement by keeping a happy mind has a lot to do with maintaining healthy diets and maintaining physical activity.

Did you know that keeping a happy mind is good for memory?

There are diverse ways to improve your memory by spending time with friends and laughing!

Have Good Friends... or a Dog.

Humans are very social as a species. In reality, engaging with others is very important in our lives: it serves as an encouragement for our brains and improves memory. Evidence has shown that people with a busy social life have shown a slower memory loss. Good memory strategies also include joining a club, hanging out with friends, or owning a puppy!

Laugh More

Laughter is not only good for our emotional well-being, but it also improves memory. Many emotions affect only certain brain areas. Nevertheless, laughter affects other countries.

It can also stimulate the mind at an intellectual level, for instance, if you need a joke. You can use humor to boost your memory in many ways:

Entertain if anyone laughs: find out what the joke is!

Smile with yourself: make funny rather than painful, embarrassing moments.

Hang out and see the bright side of life with light-hearted people.

Write a funny book or find amusing online stories.

Keep surrounded by books, such as dumb photos or posters.

Relax More

Relaxation is a good memory improvement tip. You're probably happier if you're more confident. If you have long periods of pressure, this can be very harmful to your brain: it can destroy the cells and also damage your hippocampus in the memory-keeping area.

There are a variety of memory improvements that can help control stress. For example,* Meditation has been proven scientifically to improve memory.

This is because it helps reduce anxiety and depression and physical conditions, including hypertension and diabetes, when it comes to stress. Meditation also helps to improve focus, creativity, and learning.

Meditation affects the brain physically in several ways: it strengthens the left prefrontal cortex, a part of the brain that focuses on pleasure, it allows the brain to create more neural relations, and it extends the cortex.

Yoga is another tool used to relieve stress and, therefore, a practice that can be used to improve memory. It uses several fixed positions and deep respiratory exercises to calm the body and brain.

There are lots of techniques to choose from for memory improvement. Just go online for a variety of methods to boost your memory.

The body and mind are interlinked, and how you feel impacts you as a whole seriously. Even feeling better and more comfortable will help to improve your memory. Such strategies will not only help you to remember but will also make you feel good!

CHAPTER 20

Memory Improvement Games

As you grow up, your memory capacity always deteriorates. It is difficult to remember names, telephone numbers, and other items.

Although this is a normal thing, it can also be avoided. If you want to prevent this scenario, start using memory-improving games to take steps to overcome this solvent epidemic.

That's why you purchase this book because you want to know more about this subject. You'd also know where to find these games that boost your memory. This would certainly save you from the difficulties of looking for ways to find games that boost your memory.

You don't just have to go anywhere else to find it. This chapter contains all the necessary things that you need to know about this topic. I find this to be my favour to you.

And when you finish reading this page, I'm sure you'd have a concrete idea of how to find those memory improvement games that you undoubtedly have to boost your memory.

I won't go anywhere else. I would take a glass of soda and read this chapter if I were you.

If you are concerned about your loss of memory due to old age, you can best play memory-improving games for this. This would certainly help the brain to access all the required information easily and much faster than normal. Most of the information is in your brain; your ability to remember it is a problem.

To boost these, play a few memory improving games and watch the memory deficit miraculously recover. In a short time, you would see better results, and this would also lead to better performance at work and at school and at home. You would also be a better person and a much more trustworthy person.

Now, where are these players for performance improvement?

Okay, the easiest way to find something is by logging in to the internet. Millions of internet sites offer different types of memory-improving games and are particularly tailored for any age group in which you reside. Most of these games can be downloaded free of charge.

You also have a lot of options to choose from; you can even play another game every day. This game's memory will give you lots of fun moments and give you the benefit to strengthen and develop your memory, unlike what you used to do.

Your memory is dynamic and constantly changing skillset. And while memory capacities are going to decrease slowly as we age, there is a range of effective techniques to avoid deterioration.

All five senses contribute to the development and preservation of your brain. Think each of the five senses to demonstrate them: hearing, seeing, feeling, touching, and smelling.

We can use an example of how every sense allows you to remember. You can recall the sounds of a train whistle, and also remember what a train looks like. You can remember vividly what your grandmother's house felt as she prepared a holiday party, and remember the taste of the desserts that she baked.

And while all five senses help to create our memory, our brain compiles all the different images, sounds and text, allowing us to get information on request. The best way to help the brain run at full strength is to make it know with proven scientific methods.

But you can stimulate your brain in other ways, such as playing brain teaser games or just doing proper training for your brain. There's a reason why crossword puzzles are so popular here are our top three brain games to help improve your brainpower and memory.

It is a challenge for us to recall vocabulary elements and a predefined fit within the context of the puzzle. The vocabulary is a memory factor so that any practice that improves the vocabulary improves your memory as well.

It is a good idea to start with a puzzle-like exercise and then move on to the more difficult. This technique is a good way to build your overall mental ability and help your brain learn.

Activities that help you link one word or phrase to another are also a good choice.

Word Association

The old "Password" TV show is a perfect example. While a guessing factor is involved, the hint encourages the brain to think of different options. Furthermore, successful hints are another great brain exercise. Essentially, you need to note which particular clue helps your partner formulate the right response.

There are hundreds of online and offline word association games available. These are especially fun as they can be played individually as opposed to in a group setting.

Scientists of the Image Association found that objects were probably the most important cause for memory. Most brain training programs, in reality, teach students to associate an image with something they would like to recall.

Since images are so effective in the overall memory improvement process, object association games will boost your memory. A good example is the "Pictionary" game, in which players try to determine the picture. Even the time tested.

Charade game is an enjoyable brain training game, as it challenges you to remember the song, film and book titles, description. The most important thing to improve your memory is to improve your mind and to recall details on request.

While it's a complex process, you can help keep your brain healthy by avoiding memory loss. An enjoyable experience such as the above games is preferable because you are more likely to take part in a fun process than in traditional memorization or other less engaging methods.

Get a magazine and browse around for a minute at the images or short sentences. Then open the magazine and try to write what you saw. You can write down what things you just saw for the photo. Just write down all the words you can recall for the paragraphs.

If you perform poorly in this game, don't be demotivated. You will find that you will get better and better with training. Compare the results you had initially with your current progress after a while. Your memory changes will give you a great boost in confidence.

What you do is train your brain to recall details in a short time. When your brain gets used to this process, it knows what is needed and will always strive to do it better. The brain is the most complex and powerful organ in the body. Without much effort, it can learn to do tricks and better itself. You have to perform the tasks you have set for it.

If you want to boost your memory, reading books on improving your IQ is important. The books have plenty of activities, and you have to do them and play them as a player. There are many more IQ questions and puzzles you can read on the internet.

The games you play in the IQ books increase your IQ. But they also help you develop your brain and increase your memory. The ability to collect and collect information is directly related to our minds. When we say we want to improve our memory, we want to strengthen our minds.

The more games you play with your mind, the better it gets as you practice it. Improving memory starts with the fundamentals that care for your brain first.

CHAPTER 21

Practice-Based Memory Improvement

To get more benefits in life; better memory is very critical. With a better memory, you will pass all tests for outstanding credentials and be at the top of your class.

If you are working, you should recall your entire sales report, send it before your older people (without any graphs), and predict promotion and a salary increase. Or you can always dial 911 in case of an emergency, which is easy to remember so far.

But how can we boost our memory and stay focused on our lives?

Several people studied different methods to improve memory, such as imagining and comparing images, making realistic and amusing images, converting digits to picture words to "associate" things in a lengthy sequence to the roster, and matching objects with linking words to recall numbers.

These are several conventional methods, which can be found on the internet from different memory guides. Although there are some terminology and system variations, the fundamental principles are identical.

Even with these recall methods in mind, there are tremendous possibilities that such techniques cannot be used to remember chemical laboratory equations. You can use other techniques to boost your memory to help. There are ways to focus on a particular application. The trick is to use and maintain the methodology and the information you have already studied.

If you have learned these techniques, you can use them almost instantly in your daily life to help you remember things more. Nevertheless, if you are serious about improving the capacity of your brain to maintain information at a higher level, you might want to try and learn more about the memory.

The best way to retain the information is to practice it constantly by repeating the item until you can research it from the heart. You should start practicing memory every day.

For example, if somebody has taught you how to drive a car and you have studied the manual, you have learned all about driving a car, which is not a good driver. This means that you know what is needed, but you must practice understanding.

Similarly, you will continue to practice your preferred memory techniques. You would likely find it difficult to create an image of objects and also may not have heard yet about which pictures are best for you.

Start your environment to find items that are easily remembered, such as contact numbers of your partner, favorite food, classmates ' email, French language, animals ' scientific names, credit card numbers, etc. Go for it!

If you find it hard to recall at any moment, never give up. Only note that if you concentrate on something, you can find some way to achieve your goal.

CHAPTER 22

Memory Improvement Through Association

———⟡———

Many psychologists agree that the brain can collect unlimited information. According to them, our brains can never burst at the seams.

It is, however, possible that the new information will conflict with the information preserved for a long time and tediously recall the older information. To avoid this type of scenario, a person should arrange the information inside him/herself.

Memory can be categorized as short-or long-term. In a short time, the brain retains information that can last for a few minutes. This kind of memory is normal and sensitive.

The brain is conditioned to throw it out quickly. At least seven short memories can be kept in mind. This is an estimate because you usually remember your cell number, but when shopping online, you need your credit card.

You don't need to do much research in the short term, such as recalling your dental check time or the name of the local priest to call for your child's baptism. This is because the knowledge is not necessarily necessary and can be overlooked.

In the case of long-term memory, on the other hand, such as a reminder of trivia contests, contact numbers, safety policies numbers, etc., additional measures must be made, because these items are important for lasting recovery.

This can be achieved during the day several times. Then try to remember the new information for at least a few weeks at a time. At the end of the retrieval cycle, the things that you recalled were permanently stored in mind.

Several techniques have been studied to improve memory, for example, object processing and association, accurate and humorous pictures, converting numbers into picture word "associating" objects in long series for listing and matching items with peg words to recall enumerated lists. Such approaches are very similar, although there are some terminological and system differences, fundamental understanding is related.

Even because of these recall methods, these techniques cannot be used to remember chemical formulas for the test. You can use some tricks to boost your memory to help.

There are ways to focus on a particular application. The trick is to use the methodology and information that you have learned and to use in your mind.

The main thing to remember is that connections and links have to be formed to retrieve hard information that will support a person's memory. This is why anyone with an average brain can remember items with mnemonics dramatically.

As an example, a person is required to remember more during the development of a Memory Temple by associating objects to other objects such as feelings, mental hits, etc. The more mental links are formed, the more chances you remember the details.

Memory is an exceptional brain process to recall things we have learned or tested. This very basic definition is unusual as it includes complex functions that integrate different brain regions and work rigorously.

CHAPTER 23

Memory Improving Techniques - Lists Made Simple

Recalling a list of unconnected objects can be a difficult task for your memory, depending on their weight (not your mind!).

Forget about getting a pen and paper, after only learning once; you can learn how to recall long lists easily and quickly. Does it sound like an ability that could be useful to you?

Read on to learn simple techniques for improving memory.

Here's a list of 10 items and look at how many things you recall in order:

- Chair
- Tree
- Beer
- Movie Picture
- Mat
- Apple
- Towel
- Goat

How many did you remember? How many did you remember?

5, 7?

They've been in or out of sequence?

I'm not reminding you of them all, I'm guessing.

I will now share a powerful technique with you that helps you to recall the list in or out of 1 hour, 1 day and 1 week without any difficulty.

We will use a memory device known as **HOOKING**. It's a way to hook up two photos. Don't worry; I've come up with an example. We have our set of hooks first, which we never forget. We will add our list to these hooks. A simple set of hooks was to make an image of each one of the numbers 1-10 that rhymes with e.g.

- Bun (rhymes with one)
- Shoe (rhymes with two)
- Tea door Hive (as in a beehive)
- Lick (picture a tongue)
- Heaven (picture the Golden Gate)
- Bat (imagine the fisherman putting his Bate on a Hook)

All we need to do now is link our list to our hooks. This is where our methods for memory improvement come together:

- o chair (that is, imagine a chair made of buns)
- o Tip: Silly pictures are the easiest to remember!)
- o Tree (that is the shoe tree instead of the leaves)
- o Beer (think beer out of a Tea Cup)
- o Beer (think of the door opening and entering a theatre).
- o See how easy?

Try to recall numbers 2, 9, 5. It's not quick! You can use simple memory-improving methods never to lose your shopping list, to-do list, or any other list you are making again!

CHAPTER 24

Meditation for Memory Improvement

Meditation is a holistic practice that trains the body and mind to focus on calmness and tranquility. It can help change your life as it can help you control pressure, improving your ability to think calmly and rationally. Improving memory also benefits from a positive thought approach. Several ways of meditation exist.

Tratak Meditation

This one of the most popular forms of meditation.

Tratak meditation means fixed gazing, which involves focusing on a single point, is a popular method of meditation. This might be a small black circle, an entity, or a burning candle.

People are usually restless; it is quite hard for the human mind to focus for a few minutes on something.

Thanks to the restlessness of the mind and lack of concentration, stressful thoughts flow very quickly.

When gazing at a particular object, calmness and tranquility can be increased. This allows a person to focus on and relieve pressure simultaneously. It also helps to increase the strength of memory and makes the mind aware, concentrate, and conscious.

Traditional Fitness Training

This therapy has been described as a type of traditional exercise for the mind and body. This allows the brain to achieve a focus that the modern world lacks. Too many things are now occupied, their minds lose concentration, and circumstances sometimes fail to be managed. It raises tension and restlessness in the form of various symptoms of stress.

Tratak meditation is a practice of prehistory. It is a yoga type that helps the mind to focus and open the spiritual centers by awakening the divine energy sources.

In Tratak meditation, you look at an object or a certain point slowly without allowing your eyes to blink; your mind follows the direction of your eyes and calms down, and your thoughts are more concentrated. When you look at something continuously, you imagine the image even if you close your eyes.

Tratak Meditation Forms

TratakSadhana helps the mind to relax and relax for a while. Nearly 80% of cognitive energy is wasted by the chaotic nature of our emotions, and the central nervous system struggles to maintain a calm balance.

When a person reaches TratakSadhana, however, he or she slowly experience peace of mind and a sense of calmness. Therefore, all unwelcome emotions are cleared of the brain.

This method also allows an individual to obtain more energy. Three different types of sadhana tratak are essentially three different forms of mediation- inner tratak, central tratak, and outer tratak.

Inner Treatment Sadhana

This is carried out by shutting the eyes and concentrating on the center of the front. This could induce some pain that slowly diminishes as the ultimate state of relaxation is achieved.

Middle TratakSadhana

The eyes and minds should focus on a candlelight or a light point in the event of a medium, TratakSadhana. You should look at the beam of light and encourage yourself to get into the meditation deeper and deeper.

Outer TratakSadhana

This is easy and simple to do, concentrating the eyes and mind on objects like moons and stars. People with weak eyesight may not be able to do this meditation as required.

Selecting the Object for Tratak Meditation

The main factor in Tratak Meditation is the selection of an object. This can be a simple burning candle or a flame, a black dot, a single flower, or a certain sign or object. The "OM" symbol is also a good way to focus. Geometrical symbols can also be used with abstract meanings specifically designed for medicine.

You should find a cool and quiet corner of the house where you can practice Tratak meditation to maximize your benefits. The room chosen should be dry and safe. Don't get into really expensive shoes or coats because they can distract your thoughts. All you need is a convenient place to meditate.

Chair or Floor Meditation

Choosing a chair or sitting on the floor is completely yours. You need to choose the position you want, depending on the strength of your back. If you try to relieve stress and anxiety, if you meditate, you must be relaxed and comfortable.

Tratak for Anxiety

Tratak's relaxation lets you concentrate on certain issues, and your mind frees up your stress. Your focus at all stages is improving and strengthening. When you hit the ultimate level of Tratak meditation, your mind is free from all the stressors and attachments that torment you.

You talk to your subconscious as you engage in self-hypnosis, and you start to talk to yourself. This is how hypnotizers can get you to do things you wouldn't normally because they can manipulate your subconscious mind.

To make self-hypnosis the most effective, you really must believe that self-hypnosis can be used positively and helpfully and believe that it works. This belief and recognition are the most important steps in this whole process.

Once you have learned and consistently practiced the art of self-hypnosis, you will start to remember more than you have ever thought.

CHAPTER 25

Improving Your Short-Term Memory

Short-Term Memory is a problem for many. It's far too easy for us to hear something without listening too clearly. If you can do a few simple short-term memory drills, it helps without even knowing it.

The first strategy that I'll demonstrate is one you've certainly seen before, basic word association. But before you disgustingly flip this page because you already know basic word association, please let me show you the right way to do it.

If you want to remember something quickly, create a bright, enjoyable, colorful picture of it. The mind thinks about images, not words, so every word you hear, like a name, is forgotten quickly.

Pegging is the next thing. It may not have been noticed by you. It's similar to the basic word association except for creating a place for your vivid, colorful, and fun images.

Once we add it, it's like hanging your keys every day on the same lock. You would never lose your keys again if you were in that tradition. Let's do this with your new business partner "Bill" you will be shaking Bill's arm, but you will see a nice crisp, colorful dollar bill instead of his glasses.

The more you practice these two strategies, the more they are automatic. There is no need to think about it any longer. Soon it'll be like driving a car or riding a bike.

How much would it be worth remembering all your contacts ' names and preferences, and remembering everything you see or hear, literally?

There is a right and wrong way to connect basic words. It seems a little dull, and you have certainly heard about it if you have ever looked for memory improvement techniques. You could have even overlooked it. But I want you to put all this aside for now and agree that there could be a more interesting and efficient way to do it.

Some people think that Word Association is fair, but what if you forget about your Association?

This happened to me before. I take the time to recall somebody's name, and then I forget what the name is meant to refer to.

The concern was that the relationship was not strong enough and not adequately unforgettable. It must be as convincing and fascinating as an excellent movie to make the connection deep enough or memorable enough.

The way you do that is through a colorful and vibrant and animated association so that when the person whose name you want to remember goes back to you, you see him or her and easily find your connection, because it's so vivid, animated and humorous that it returns to you like a storm of a memorable nature.

For example, the name "Clarke" gives you an image of Superman. You look at the tie of Clarke and see a picture of a large red "S." The name Mary can give you an image of a wedding dress, but you have to associate the dress with Mary.

For example, when Mary wears a skirt or a jacket, you look back and see the long train on a wedding dress you've ever seen.

CHAPTER 26

Memory Improvements:
How to Remember Names

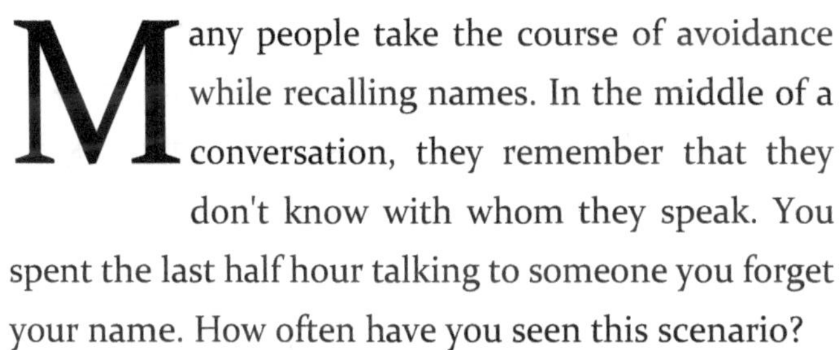

Many people take the course of avoidance while recalling names. In the middle of a conversation, they remember that they don't know with whom they speak. You spent the last half hour talking to someone you forget your name. How often have you seen this scenario?

The solution for many is to follow the clearest course: avoid the title at all costs. While this may lead to the night, it also leads to potentially unpleasant situations. 4

A better solution would be, first of all, to remember the name. Although names may be difficult to remember, the good news is that you can take a few easy steps to make it not only simple but enjoyable to remember names!

Step 1: Listen

You must first know what this name is to remember a name. Sometimes, the reason we don't remember names is because, in the first place, we never paid real attention to the word. The only way to solve this problem is to repeat your name after you've learned it.

If you skipped it, it's time to ask the person to repeat it now. In addition to repeating the name in your head, take a step further and use it aloud as soon as possible when speaking to the other person.

Step 2: Find a Substitute Word or Phrase for a Name.

This is a crucial strategy for memory improvement called replacement, not only extremely handy in every effort of memory, but also very enjoyable. You have first to assign the name some sense to help yourself remember the name. To do this, pick a word or phrase that sounds like your name.

You can imagine a walker for an older person, for example, for the last name Walker. You can imagine a martini for Martinez. Such names are quite simple, but for all names, the same method applies. There's no term you can't find a substitute for; you only have to be a bit creative.

The important thing, however odd the name may seem, is to find a replacement word that gives a vivid mental image. One rule of thumb is that larger pictures are better. Find words that give you vivid mental images and stay away from words that are fuzzy or complicated.

You can use more than one term for longer names. For example, to remember Salinski, the words "sailing" and "skis" could be used to demonstrate your sailing by skis on a ship. For your name

Besides, the words "add -a-son" can be used to construct a mental picture. The possibilities are limitless; you need to use your imagination.

Step 3: Examine the Person's Face. Is Something Sticking Out?

Test their characteristics. Do they have a crooked nose, a hairline that retreats?

Examine the eyebrows (are they bushy?) body, hair, lips, mouth, ears, etc. You are trying to find something for you. Most of the time, there's some physical character to you when you meet a person.

You want to find the element you most probably remember.

Step 4: Compare the replacement Word with the face of the person

If you do this, you are not likely to forget the name of the person. Take the replacement word and physical characteristics and build a ludicrous mental picture that includes both the word and the physical characteristics of the head.

Make sure your image is vibrant and sweet. Why is this ridiculous?

Just because you recall something amazing rather than dull,because Mr. Salinski has a nose long, you might imagine, for example, a sailboat floating down the nose with skis attached to the bottom (sailing + skiing= Salinski).

You can make yourself imaginative and see a whole line of sailboats on skis that float down and fall down your nose. When Claire has big teeth, you can imagine an illuminated tooth.

These are just a few instances, but the choice of features and the making of a vivid and exciting mental image is significant. If you do, I promise you're not going to forget a name anymore!

We all know how difficult it is to remember names, but when you follow these four steps and make a point of learning, changing, evaluating, and associating, you will have all the resources to remember your name. It takes some practice, particularly if you are not a person who naturally produces detailed mental images, but the practice is good, like anything else.

CHAPTER 27

Concentration and Memory Improvement Guidelines

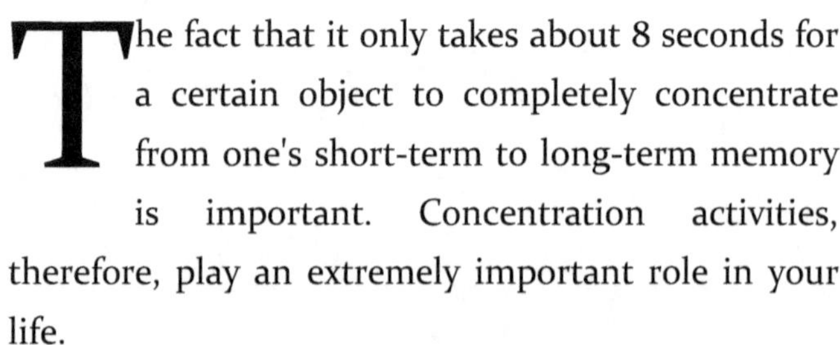

The fact that it only takes about 8 seconds for a certain object to completely concentrate from one's short-term to long-term memory is important. Concentration activities, therefore, play an extremely important role in your life.

One of the main reasons why you don't recall something is because you never really put it in your mind.

People are losing items like their house keys all the time by putting them somewhere accidentally, without paying proper attention to them. Until finally, find the lost items, such as keys, most people have to spend considerable time tracking back through the time when they have keys and don't.

Now, if you had paid attention, you would never first have lost the keys or the glasses. Researchers also tend to concentrate on learning how to increase memory and concentration. That is why one of the best ways to make a difference in your memory is to increase your focus abilities.

Therefore, you are now aware that concentration strengthens your memory, and it is a wise idea to understand the right strategies to maximize concentration. The power of the focus of any person can be increased by introducing two items.

Just increase your attention ability or make some necessary changes in your daily life to boost your memory. Yet modifying the setting to suit the concentration forces of your brain won't help in all circumstances unless you want to practice.

You will be surprised to find that your mind changes slowly as you grow older. For this purpose, it is great for you to acquire knowledge because it improves your brainpower.

So before implementing such relaxation strategies, you should change the shape of your brain. Changing your brain shape requires regular exercises that can affect your brain positively.

These include: meditation experts recommend that a person must meditate daily, including once before and once after going out of bed. After a daily routine of relaxation, you can focus much better.

Sleep

You want to sleep properly to preserve your brainpower and focus properly on issues. Make sure you sleep well every day. You can choose the mattress you use in your bed

Significantly important to the right and calming pattern of sleeping. Another thing to do is to remove the Television from your room; you don't sleep well if you go to bed while watching a show.

Most people tend to shout what they do, and what's known as a pretty effective way to boost focus. An example might be "My lenses are on my desk." TV, radio, and other gadgets can also interrupt your attention and make it difficult for you to remember things. Thus, when you do something important, you must exclude them from your presence.

Many people often try to remember the names of people they meet every day after the end of the day as a focused boost in exercise because focus improves your memory. More often than not, our clothes and looks are more important for us to hold when meeting new people.

Trying to save written text is complicated because it is hard for our brain to read it all in one go. The best way to become a better reader is by practicing more to increase your focus.

Many people often exercise focus by watching something on their TV and then asking themselves about information. You have a great brain power focus if you can remember a lot of details.

Nonetheless, most of the strategies you come across to boost your memory will show your ability to recall complex pictures and videos. Nevertheless, the capacity to focus must be limited to things that matter rather than to useless items. Sticky notes are generally a great way to remember things quickly and conveniently.

When you forget the reason you wrote it down, the power of a sticky note or document will be negated. Furthermore, while the knowledge is interpreted in many ways, you should not forget that you will know and remember the majority of what happens in front of you if you concentrate hard enough.

CHAPTER 28

Water Intake
and Memory Improvement

Most people do not realize that the intake of water is particularly important for memory improvements. Sufficient water intake keeps the body and the brain working properly. Like the skin, the brain can also dehydrate if the body doesn't have enough water.

People may feel hungry, light-headed, dry, or itchy if they don't drink the right quantity of water every day. This, in turn, leads to challenges in focusing on tasks and can lead to both depression and short-term memory issues.

Every day people have to drink about eight glasses of water. This can be increased, however, especially in warmer days and when people do some physical activities. Those who drop below the minimum water intake level may have problems with brain functions, especially in processing and remembering information required at a specific time or place.

Although people drink some other drinks during the day apart from milk, they have to realize that most of their drinks are just diuretics. Coffee, cola, beer, and wine may be included, which only makes them urinate more often and dehydrate their bodies and brains.

It is then important for people to verify that they are taking enough water and other liquids, but not diuretics. Those who do not like to drink water because it does not taste can instead try to drink cocoa milk.

According to some recent research, coconut juice is good for the body and the mind. Several studies also show that it may be a better way to keep the body and brain hydrated than food. It also provides vital nutrients that allow the body and brain to function properly.

Other considerations still need to be considered if you want to boost your memory, aside from having enough air. We also have to eat properly, sleep well, and exercise physically and mentally.

Humans should function by keeping their minds working most of the time. These will all help to increase the brain's ability to process, store, and retrieve the information required. The healthy and strong body and brain will not only allow people to keep their memories intact but will also help people to live longer lives.

Improving the brain's health is critical in the memory recovery program. Sufficient exercise helps you develop your memory. Eating mineral foods allows you to boost your memory technology. Stay active mentally, as this helps.

CHAPTER 29

Memory Improvement by Concentrating on One Thing at a Time

We're all aware of the way it is: so much needs to be done that it seems we have to work together to do it. But what do we do to our brain if we do a lot of work?

Too much can slow you down by up to 50% and cause enormous pressure to the brain. You are much less effective during multi-tasking. And a break between many things may cause short-term memory loss.

We all do it, of course. Sometimes it's also required–especially if you've got a lot of people demanding your time. Only ask any small children's mother!

But it's NOT needed most of the time. And generally, it's counterproductive.

What is crazy is that multi-tasking does not get things done faster! When you try to do two things at once, your brain automatically turns off one job temporarily while concentrating on the other. The mind can only function on one task at a time.

And multitasking doesn't save you any time. This gives you the impression of improved productivity, but your work is of great quality. While doing other things, the ability to store new memories is SEVERY blurred.

Reports show that even multi-tasking attempts can reduce your cognitive abilities. Bombarding the brain with several information sources can make it difficult to focus, to recall, or to move from work to work. Multitask people are often easily distracted because the mind cannot handle more than one string of information at a time.

Intense multitasking, according to different studies and brain scans, causes stress in your body in the form of an adrenaline rush that can damage brain cells.

Short-term memory loss can be an alert to avoid multiple tasks and focus your attention on one thing at a time. The management of two or more tasks concurrently reduces the brainpower to one task, while sustained concentration and attention allow long-term memory absorption.

Every time you juggle two or more things at once note that this does not only lead to poor quality jobs but could also be very detrimental to the health of your brain. The trick is to eliminate obstacles and focus on one thing at a time.

Exercises to Improve the Performance of Your Brain

For most people, knowing memory and doing memory improvement exercises is not a matter of much concern–before they know that they start to slip. This is caused by many factors, such as age, stress, and other lifestyles.

Not everyone has an inherent ability to recall essential facts and information. The good news is that these skills can be mastered, and your memory improved. Whether you are a young college student or reaching your golden years, these five simple tricks help keep your mind alive.

1. Just Sing a Song.

How often did you sit at a red light or in the office of a doctor and hear a song in your head? If you are lucky, it's sweet, but it's just as likely you'll hear a bit of irritating ditty somewhere.

While you may have some strategies to eliminate this unwanted stuff from your mind, the better approach is to use this linking force for your benefit. Your brain is designed to recall with art.

Set it to music if you have a list of things you have to recall or a table of information. In reality, choose your most mysterious song–the one that pops up most often in these unguarded moments–and use it as your musical association. This is one of the activities that anyone of any age can do to strengthen the memory.

2. The Mind Loves a Good Game, Play Games.

Thankfully, it's great for your brain, too. The cliché of the clever old bird, spectacled and sporting a crossword puzzle, has some justification.

This character appears in mystery novels and movies over and over again. In reality, playing mental games keeps your mind and brain-healthy in your golden years. Items like Sudoku, Scrabble, and other phrases, numbers, and reminder games are great.

3. Check Yourself

We all have memory tricks that help to keep us on track. The use of these methods is nothing wrong. Don't be too reliant on them, though, or your memory function will decline.

Use the memory aids instead to check yourself. For example, when you make a food list, take it to you, but try to see how many things you can remember without mentioning the list. Make your target every time you do this exercise to boost your performance.

4. The Family

Association has always been a trick used for those with active minds. Most people are impressed by a skill that can always add to the interaction of a personal touch by holding names in mind.

Most of these spouses have no magic trick to do this. Alternatively, they connect that person with a mental picture that they already know. This simple technique encourages the mind to be involved.

5. Relationships Matter

This may sound like an out-of-place classification of memory improvement. Memory, however, has a close relationship with feelings and relationships.

In reality, a dementia patient is normal to remember events based on smells, sights, or the environment. This is an emotional connection in many situations. Relationships of value will keep your memory intact throughout your life.

For people who think they're likely to forget or have memory problems later in life or who may already experience these difficulties, it's never too late for the brain to improve by doing some exercises to improve the memory.

Contrary to popular beliefs, you can teach new ideas to your mind. Neuroplasticity can be literarily defined as the brain's ability to construct new neural pathways. Also known as cortical repair, this mechanism is the way the brain changes because of the experiences of a person.

One great memory exercise that we all do every day is to socialize with others, families, and friends. You can make a point of calling a friend or parent every day to catch each other up.

You can also plan to join a team or club, volunteer, or meet new like-minded people. Several respondents also said they had positive experiences with a new dog or cat. We are very social animals and are a great medium for meeting new people.

There's nothing like a good joke that stimulates the brain. It tests attention very powerfully. Whatever makes you laugh is great medicine for your brain. Laughter activates a significant part of the brain and induces the release of neuroplastic chemicals.

The ingenuity involved with making a good joke or remembering a fine, humorous repertoire is an excellent exercise in memory and brainpower. Seek out people with whom you can smile, or who can make you laugh.

I still recommend meditation as an outstanding memory improvement practice. It's an unbeatable way to teach yourself to concentrate, focus, and block distractions. These are basic skills for those with excellent memory skills.

Meditation helps activates the left prefrontal cortex of the brain that is the same region of pleasure. Meditation also strengthens the interaction between the brain hemispheres.

A crucial step to take when trying to improve your memories is to remove negative influences that inhibit the memory function of the brain. Depression is one such element.

The disease drains the body from the energy and leaves little to normal, healthy brain activity. When you feel you might be depressed, you should seek professional medical treatment for the condition, and your memory will surely improve dramatically.

Nutrition is another field where we can improve as individuals to promote a healthy mind and memory. Try to start with a balanced diet that is low in saturated fats and cholesterol and will certainly improve brain health.

Better brain circulation ensures it will work more efficiently. Foods that are high in fatty acids from Omega 3 are good for the brain's health and can even help prevent Alzheimer's.

Memory tests don't just have to be "conscious." You should also include physical training in your memory, improving the program. The overall health of your body can affect your mental health tremendously. Try to integrate all these techniques and, when you mature in your later years, you will have a powerful and strong mind.

CHAPTER 31

Adult Friendly Memory Exercises

Most people are taking care of not only their physical health but also their mental health. The great news is that there are tons of exercises to improve the memory of a person, which are both effective and fun.

Memorization does not always mean that large quantities of information or trivial numbers are recalled. Fun to check your memory by playing a list of your favorite old school songs and repeating the words to see how much you recall.

This kind of memory exercise is perfect for adults aged the 20s, 30s, 40s, and over regardless of whether the choices came out two years ago or 20 years ago.

You will not only know how good your memorization is, but also the best way to jump up and dance, sing along and recall where you were when every song came out. Do this event along the memory lane with your closest friends.

Flashcards with Twist

Flashcards have been popular for years, but why not use them as a space improvement exercise to your advantage?

Make your flashcards, but choose a subject that you do not know before. To make things more interesting. You want to pick a topic that is not dull.

Perhaps you have always wanted to find out more about the culture of a certain country, find out who holds the most out of the record worlds, or learn biographies of some of your favorite historical figures.

Regardless of the topic, collect as much information as possible and divide it too easy concepts for each flashcard. Each time you feel the need, take them out and see how much you can recall.

Would you like to make your next visit to the food shop memorable?

Challenge yourself by doing memory improvement drills that allow you to save your food list instead of a written list. Parents can even have fun with their kids.

Write down your item list and send it to your boys. Once you hit the food shop, see how many items you can recall and add to your cart, your children must keep your list back during this period... no cheating!

Before you go to the check-out booth, have your children check your products for what you have written on the list. Grocery shopping is never going to be boring again!

Remember the days when all of us can remember every one of our family and friend's telephone numbers?

Don't get distracted with your smartphone and your software, take it on yourself to list about 10 telephone numbers you frequently use and commit the number to the memory every time you manually instead of using the phone's built-in address book. If you memorize a set of 10 numbers effectively, add 10 more to store and so on.

Nice to Meet You

Even people with the best memories often have difficulty remembering the names of people they knew. To make things more interesting, and introducing a new form of memory improvement, try to remember not only the name of the person you have just met but also list 3 or 4 things you inform of.

This kind of memory is very useful because it helps you when you next try to remember the name of a person. If required, write down the information using flashcards and check yourself periodically, because this approach can be particularly useful for those in the business world who are frequently exposed to new people.

CHAPTER 32

Nutrition and Memory Improvement

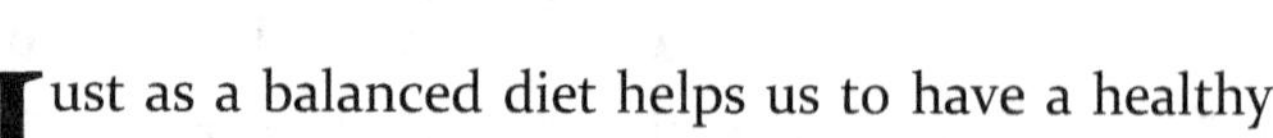

Just as a balanced diet helps us to have a healthy body, so it does improve memory.

There are several factors in our daily lives, such as stress, anxiety, depression, sleeplessness, and hormonal imbalances that can adversely affect our health and mind.

All these factors can lead to poor focus, deteriorating ability, and decreased learning capacity, which are essential indicators of a bad memory. The good news is, though, that, along with some other tips on improving memory, healthy diets will help you battle this.

Nutrients that help improve memory: vitamins and minerals A variety of vitamins and minerals contribute significantly to the improvement of memory.

- o   Vitamin A helps to combat harmful toxins that can kill cells of the brain.

- o   Vitamin B1 and pantothenic acid help to produce acetylcholine, a product for the brain cell that helps to reduce the levels of concentration.
- o   B3 contributes to the overall health of the brain, while B6 improves nerve interaction.
- o   Vitamin B12 plays a vital role in the acceleration of electrical nerve transmission by leading to the growth of the nerve defense myelin sheath.
- o   Folic acid helps to prevent Alzheimer's disease from progressing.
- o   Vitamin C leads to the elimination of free radicals that can kill the brain cells.
- o   Vitamin E allows the brain to function better.
- o   Selenium improves vitamin E action.
- o   Zinc helps to improve memory while iron improves concentration.

Certain nutrients for memory improvement

Several other nutritional and health supplements can improve your memory a bit. Look:

- o Apple Juice-Recent studies show that apple juice can help prevent Alzheimer's disease, which is linked to age memory loss.

---

o Fish Oils and Fish — DMAE, a most essential chemical commonly found in fish, contributes to the production of acetylcholine that leads to an increase in concentration.

However, fresh vegetables, fruits, and low-fat dairy products can be used to improve memory. All these factors can lead to poor focus, loss of abilities, and poor learning capacity, which are important indicators of poor memory.

The good news is that along with other tips to improve memory; a healthy intake will help you to overcome this. Just as the diet allows us to have a healthy body, it also helps to improve our memory.

Special Vitamins

The food we consume sometimes does not contain enough vitamins to maintain a healthy brain.Supplementation with vitamins can make up for this food deficit and help improve your memory. Although all of the vitamins are important, some play a unique role in improving your memory, and you most need them if you have troublesome memory.

1. Vitamin E.

Vitamin E is best known for its antioxidant properties and prevents nerve damage due to a lack of oxygen to your brain. The vitamin also prevents memory loss associated with age.

Vitamin E has been shown to boost an old memory. Other studies show that Alzheimer's disease is avoided and that it is delaying development among people who suffer from it already.

2. B6 vitamin. It helps to improve memory by using it always. Vitamin B6 also speeds up the ability of the brain to store and retain information.

3. B9 vitamin. This vitamin, also known as folic acid, stimulates the development of infected blood cells that deliver oxygen and nutrients to the brain. Folic acid also reduces the rate of memory loss.

4. B12 vitamin. This works differently from vitamins B6 and B9. A drug, as compared to them, reduces homocysteine levels. Homocysteine amino acids are associated with poor brain function.

Vitamin B12 is also unique in terms of its ability to repair damaged nerve fibers. It is better paired with vitamin B6 when you wonder how your performance can be improved.

5. Vitamin C. An antioxidant, like vitamin E, is also present. It can help defend you from memory loss because of old age and other causes.

6. Vitamin D. This void prevents the formation of new memories in your mind. Vitamin D deficiency in older people is associated with memory loss. Specific nutrients should help you reduce these issues and improve your memory.

Your sure-fire means to keep a strong memory is a balanced meal of fruits, vegetables, and nutritious food. There are many benefits of eating the right food to provide you with the nutrients you need to spend time learning.

Herbs that Help Improve the Memory

Many forms of herbs help improve memory. One may wonder whether this is true or not, but herbs have been used for the improvement of memory since ancient times. Various spices or spicy foods improve the cognitive functions of the brain.

In reality, people can buy them in their shops or local markets. You could have used these spices or herbs in the preparation and cooking of your dishes without realizing the positive effects on brain improvement.

Turmeric

People who love food made with curry using turmeric. Curcumin is the element in turmeric, which helps to improve memory. It also helps to reduce the incidence of brain diseases like Alzheimer's.

Ginger

The ginger is one of the herbs that help to improve memory. The Zingerrone material of ginger strengthens the brain's nerves, which can function very well and improve memory.

Cinnamon This special spice will help the memory grow because the taste activates the brain to release chemicals that activate a good mood.

Gingko Biloba

It is believed that this herb can improve blood flow into the brain. The proper blood flow provides the brain more oxygen needed to function properly.

Gotu Kola This is another herb that helps memory develop. It also helps to reduce the chances of developing senility, most especially for older people.

Siberian Ginseng

This herb can help the body cope with stress by fostering nervous system control. It also provides the body with strength to combat tiredness and stress.

While these herbs and spices can improve memory, people have to do their work. You may also explore the impact of these herbs on brain development with their health care providers.

Something excess is always risky, but one thing is certain. People can boost their memory through the food they eat. A well-balanced diet can fuel the body and allow the brain to function correctly.

Other things can help people to improve their memory.

Memory recovery includes physical and mental exercises. The brain must be activated properly. Although some of the herbs can help improve memory, people can balance it with important items such as good food and regular workouts.

CHAPTER 33

Memory Improvement Medications

Many treatments improve people's ability to think and recall, in particular, those with Alzheimer's disease or other mental illnesses. Those who are sometimes well may also want to take some memory improvement medications even if they don't have to.

For example, students can take these memory pills to meet the demands of their academic studies. Although the memory capacity may be improved, those without mental illness or disease must seek the advice of medical experts before taking any form of memory-improving drugs.

There is still insufficient evidence to show that taking some memory-improving drugs will improve brain functions in healthy individuals. If there would ever be some memory medication put on the market, people should ensure that it has been checked and is approved by the FDA.

For example, nootropics are used by individuals to improve their cognitive functions. The medication is expected to modify the number of neurochemicals in the brain and also increases the oxygen supply and also promotes nerve production. Individuals may have some signs of mild side effects.

There may be a variety of other drugs that people use in their ability to concentrate and to retrieve information, apart from Nootropics, but again, these drugs are primarily used to treat people such as people who need to minimize their impulsive behavior.

Individuals may consider taking vitamin supplements to help their brains work properly, but they may not necessarily have health safety or effectiveness before they become sold out on the market, just as memory improves medications. Dietary supplements can be taken, but booking appointments with physicians should be safer first.

Vitamins B, Omega 3, IsoFlavones, Vitamin D, and Gingko Biloba are some of the supplements that are marketed to improve cognitive functions. If people take medications or vitamins and supplements for memory improvement, they weren't informed that they could improve their brain function.

Most of these items still need to be tested for efficacy and safety. People should analyze their diets and the kind of rest and sleep they take when considering medications or dietary supplements.

They can also analyze their physical and mental exercises because these are some natural ways to increase brain functions, particularly in the processing and collection of information.

Improving your brain's health is synonymous with improving your memory. Sufficient exercise helps you with increasing your memory. Mineral foods help you improve memory capacity.

CHAPTER 34

How to Get a Photographic Memory

Although a few people are injured with an excellent memory, most people have an average memory at best. But you can take a specific course to get a photographic memory...

You may have seen examples of a photographic memory, usually on late-night television. A person often demonstrates his outstanding memory skills by reciting deck cards in perfect order or similar features.

And it might sound like magic or trick, but it isn't. Many people have memories of photography, and it is almost always due to special training techniques. Luckily, these training methods are not extremely costly or time-consuming and are open to nearly everyone.

Photographic memory is a brain function and how visual information is stored. The brain can store photos or even words on a page and recall information on demand. It's a highly developed skill, but in fact, we all have the same ability.

The memory is a brain function and the five senses. We can recall and retrieve information based on images, sounds, tastes, emotions, and smells. Sadly, it is not enough to have an acute sense of smell and excellent vision as it relates to memory. The brain must communicate with the senses in order to improve memory skills.

Your sight and mind will need to function together to develop a photographic memory. Perfect vision is not required, but a highly skilled mind.

You have to train your brain to memorize whether you want a photographic memory or to improve your memory. Some simple exercises, like card tricks and crossword puzzles, are available. Both behaviors lead to calming the mind, but not long-term remedies.

The explanation is that they allow you to find information on request in specific activity overtraining the mind.

You have to train it, just as you would a muscle, to teach and prepare the brain to respond upon request. We propose a system of brain training using a building block approach. After all, holding information is complicated, and a training program must, as it were, be conducted in bits of bite-size.

A typical training system for the brain is machine bases, usually available in a DVD format or better on request. It usually takes about 12 weeks and can be completed at your rate at your own time.

Some elements of the curriculum concentrate on spatial relationships and visual remembering. The exercises are enjoyable and engaging, allowing you to learn while developing your memory skills. You can, for instance, be asked to identify several forms and then place them in the order you see them.

The task may include the combination of forms with words or forms with objects, which improves the ability to process images in order. As you can imagine, the work begins relatively simple and then grows in complexity with your expertise.

As long as the training takes, you will experience a significant improvement in your memory, regardless of your age. Memory is a talent like any other skill, such as playing the piano or running a marathon, when you think about that. Excellent skills take practice and preparation.

Preparation.

So, you have a photographic memory after you have completed a brain training program? Although it is quite probable, it will probably require further training and practice. Yet one thing is sure. It will dramatically improve your ability to recall names, dates, directions, and faces.

The acquisition of photographic memory is an ability to remember images and to recover them on request. Try engaging in a brain training program designed to improve your memory skills. Such programs are inexpensive, smooth, and use a component approach to develop your knowledge.

CHAPTER 35

Stress Control and Improving Memory

Our society has changed more rapidly than our genes. Nowadays, instead of facing real and immediate life-threatening emergencies that require instant action, we face events and diseases which are slowly coming upon us, stressing us and damaging our brain and memory.

Humans can "stress them with thinking; they can respond to the same pressure as zebra." But zebra releases the stress hormones employing lifelong practice, while generally, we tend to muddle, becoming more nervous at the moment.

What is the relation between stress and memory?

We all know that our brain, weight, and mood are bad for chronic stress, but how do we remember?

Ironically, acute stress can help you focus more clearly and remember things. Chronic stress, on the other hand, decreases the concentrating ability and can directly affect the hippocampal cells, a brain structure important for short-term memory encoding.

When is it normal to have stress?

When you feel unable to control your life, you may feel anxious or irritable. Because everyone changes the type and amount of pressure in their response, there are some things you can do to feel more informed about your climate. A sense of empowerment will reduce stress and strengthen your memory.

Yoga, mindfulness, and visualizations are good ways to manage stress levels. Reducing stress and stress hormones are important to your brain and overall fitness in your body.

What are the best ways to protect our minds and remembrances from chronic stress?

1-Learning improves the body and can reduce stress, depression, and anxiety experience. Make sure you do cardiac things at least twice a week.

2-Calm relaxation, tai chi, yoga, or any other methods to lower blood pressure, slow breathing, slow metabolism, and muscle tension. Grant yourself 10 minutes every day to relax.

3-Biofeedback apps and games that provide information in real-time to help you learn effective strategies to reduce stress.

4-Empowerment because behaviors of personal confidence and environmental control overcome tension. Make sure you and the support group around you appreciate the good things you've done and done.

5-Friends, family, and pets' social networking help build trust, encouragement, and relaxation.

6-Use a calendar to schedule important matters. Give a date and priority to products.

7-Make a list of the things to do. Even if it's a long list, it can be rewarding to complete things.

8-Ask yourself how important it is for you. Maybe you're worrying something you'd better let go.

9-Get enough rest for your batteries to recharge.

10-Eat well and reduce your intake of caffeine and sugar that may contribute to your sense of jitteriness.

These are not miracle remedies but habitual behaviors that improve memory and quality of life.

CHAPTER 36

Improved Human Memory and Neuro-Nutrition

Some interesting new ways to boost your memory are found in the new field of nutritional neuroscience and neuro-nutrition. We start thinking about foods and food supplements as drugs is a new way of approaching what we consume, and there is no place where it is more important than the brain.

It's fascinating for you when you think about what this tiny body, the size of your two hands, holds together. It is our home, our vision, our problem-solving skills, and our memory.

It is an amazing organ that needs care just as our bodies and hearts do. It needs care. Are you aware that the brain's wellbeing is 70% natural (including the nutrients you add) and only 30% genetically engineered?

Let's see how our minds and brains can be changed.

The diet of our ancient ancestors is good for our brains and also strengthens our souls. It makes sense to think of it as the human body is continuous, though gradually transforming into the best' tool' to cope with the world.

The diet "stone age" influenced the developing brain at the time and also set the parameters for what the brain required and could handle. Life for an individual was quite different at this time but remained the same for many centuries before the advent of commercial agriculture became the standard.

Since then, life has changed dramatically over a very short time. Our minds and bodies lag far behind our modern lifestyle. To help our bodies return to the original state and survive again, we need a large scale of ancient food and a less proportion of modern processed food.

What the wild game is, wild fish, wild plants, nuts, baits, and roots! What is the wild game? Our bodies have now been bombarded with older foods-not to mention alcohol and isolated fats-like refined grains, sugar, and milk products. Oops!

It does not look easy to thrive on such different foods for our brains. Especially if you know that 83% of our food is' fresh' and 17% old. New ancestors used to eat thrice the number of fruits and vegetables and ten times the amount of protein!

The major difference was the change in the sort of oils that they drink. We need Omega 3 and omega 6, but they need to be about the same. We drink 20 times as much omega-6 as omega-3.

The brain cells can't do well with this system, and in this case, they shut down or malfunction badly. Omega-3 oils are obtained from wild meat, oily fish, and some animal products. Omega 6 oils are made from maize butter, margarine, and baked goods.

So...

Take good care of your mind and make these changes to your diet. It must last for your life and if you know what it needs.

Make the majority of your meals, fruits, and vegetables–eat nuts, especially almonds and walnuts once allergies have been tested.

Eat fatty fish such as salmon, sardines and mackerel, shell-fish (a test of allergies again)-eat game, and skin-free white meat.

Don't consume lots of sugar and salt-don't eat lots of fried food before it's put into a microwave container-take vitamins and mineral supplements-take the capsules of fish oil if you don't eat fish more than two days a week.

CHAPTER 37

Memory Improvement Strategies to Help You Succeed in Life

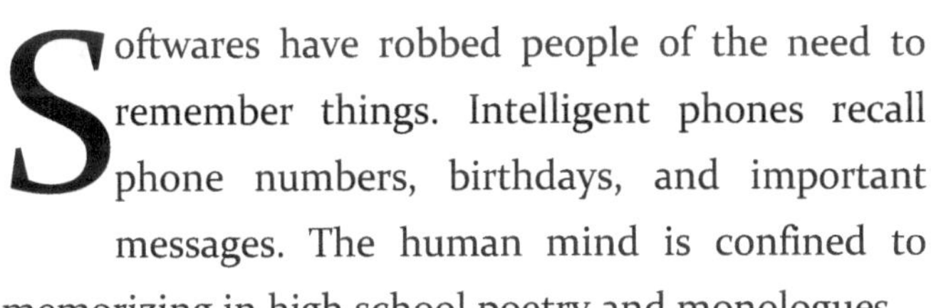

Softwares have robbed people of the need to remember things. Intelligent phones recall phone numbers, birthdays, and important messages. The human mind is confined to memorizing in high school poetry and monologues.

While it is true that these devices have made life uncomplicated and straightforward, they have created an environment that, without them, it is impossible to imagine!

Even the toughest gadget freak needs to boost his memory. Several studies show that interventions that help improve the memory of Alzheimer's and other forms of dementia can delay successfully.

Apart from devices such as cell phones and computers, several other factors cause people with memory problems. Memory problems are usually caused by physical, psychological, and emotional factors. Stress and strain often adversely affect the ability of the brain to recall information.

If people were computers, memory improvement would require additional storage chips. Nevertheless, the retrieval process for information in humans is slightly more complicated than computers.

Memory loss can cause serious problems with equally serious consequences. Whether you are a businessman, a student, or a businessman, poor memory can cause major job disturbances.

While computers are currently available to store the most valuable information, they cannot be used to store and manage each piece of information. Memory changes are important, and the change process needs to be very concentrated and results-oriented.

The memory cells are like the body's muscles. You should train them and feed them with adequate nutrition to grow well and stay healthy. Some organized online games and processes can serve as excellent strategies to improve memory.

You need to use your memory to boost memory cell output. Also, there are some simple instructions that you can follow to improve your memory. As you all know, your memory loss could be attributed to certain faulty behaviors that you have been following unconsciously for years.

Improvement of memory: Basic corrective actions

Some basic corrective actions to improve memory can be discussed under the following headings. If you do not recall things that have already been presented to you over some time, a lack of focus or concentration may be the main culprit.

The brain requires approximately 8 seconds to focus on storing a piece of information. When you can't concentrate too long, get rid of all distractions and try to concentrate on improving retention.

To rapidly improve your memory, you have to use trial and error techniques to deduce your desired learning style and stick to it. Many people keep knowledge longer through visual sensory strategies such as watching a video or reading. Others might consider the auditory style to be more successful when listening to a recording of lectures. Track your performance and choose the best way.

It is very important that you can associate raw information with pieces of information you already know and that both information types are effectively remembered. One better way to remember items is to build a series in your memory like a string.

Here one reality attracts the other immediately, and you end up recalling everything in one aspect. The next time you try to hold something, add it to something extremely familiar to you. It would make knowing it very convenient.

Organized in Your Approach

If you intend to retain information, it is very important to be organized in your approach. Whether documents, records, statements, or diaries, it is necessary to arrange them properly so that you can refer as and when needed to the appropriate areas. It will simplify the whole recruitment cycle by all means.

You can't just boost your memory. It is, however, important that your brain constantly improves its skills by including them in intellectually stimulating activities and games and combining adaptable memory changes with tips and exercises on an everyday routine.

Memory methods are commonly referred to as mnemonics. Mnemonics allow people with poor memories to retrieve information quickly.

Mnemonics changes the shape of the memories into something that the brain can save and absorb quickly. Mnemonics uses all kinds of skills, like your smell, sound, vision, emotions, etc.

Three factors determine mnemonics: imagination, interaction, and place. Imagination is one of the most important mnemonics variables. For strong imagination, it's simpler by committing them to memory to visualize scenarios. A vivid imagination can contribute to memories easier to absorb and recall from a human brain.

On the other hand, the association is a strategy of vital importance in the production of memory. This includes linking new information to previously stored information in your mind. The relation between the two memories depends on many variables, such as smell, taste, vision, sound, etc.

The position includes merging two different sets of memories according to their meaning. Example: By putting one in a city-based situation and the other in a city, there may be two distinctive memories.

All concepts are then easily separated, and any confrontation is avoided. The emotional variants in location-based memories allow the information to be richer in emotions to make it easier to process them.

If you think about memory strategies, chunking is one of the most important techniques you will ever come across. The process requires the separation of information into different groups.

It is most useful when dealing with unordered bits of information. Therefore, information is saved in numbered form by chunking. You can split the number list into as many categories as you want.

Photos can be stored in your mind very quickly. Information or information within your mind can be easily stored when you relate it to pictures. Yet make sure the picture is good.

Colorful pictures are more powerful than dull ones. Likewise, both funny and odd pictures are recommended. Your goal should also be to highlight the most important parts of the picture.

Rhyming is also a great way to improve your memory. For example, most people tend to know "Thirty days hath September." Many people access the days of the month using this particular technique. Just as before, a rude rhyme is much easier to remember than a good one.

On the other hand, most people use bridging to strengthen their memories. The technique requires the negotiation of two concepts. Your job is basically to build a bridge between two different ideas that connects them.

Similarly, acronyms are a system in which you make a larger word remembered by using the letter of any word in a sentence. You must have never used this particular technique.

It is nevertheless quite hard for you to gauge the meaning of the knowledge you memorize because the acronym helps you to cement it in your head. You cannot use acronyms for information or information structure of any kind. Often you will see that the acronym that you just created is gibberish and meaningless.

Songs are another way to memorize complex information bits. Most of the songs can be added as they go. Nonetheless, this particular approach cannot be used on all passages and is therefore restrictive. In general, mathematics educators use this particular approach to improve student memorization skills.

Bedtime recital is also very common when you know how to memorize easy. In addition to speeches, you can use it to preserve poems and scripts. Essentially, you have to read the passage several times before you go to bed. The details will be written in your mind when you wake up.

You should use these approaches as often as possible until you see signs of improvement.

Basics of Memory Retention

The preservation of memory is a fascinating subject; most people would like to understand and change in their lives. Two forms of memory exist.

A long-term memory in which knowledge and memories are retained in your mind for a long time and a short time where information is temporarily processed and is not recovered.

Here are three strategies for memory maintenance to improve memory retention in all cases.

1. Exercise Regularly

Doing exercise allows the blood to pass to all parts of the body. This, in turn, provides our muscles and body parts with oxygen to keep them healthy. Your brain needs oxygen to remain healthy and sustain optimal performance. Exercise will make you lose weight and feel more confident all day long.

If you are healthy and your mind is on the move, space dramatically improves. Your ability to remember new things and expertise, if needed, can be easily achieved.

Most people ignore drills because they do not equate them with memory improvement, but they are so right. Better memory begins with preparation, as you will then have the health and energy to work efficiently in your mind.

2. Getting Enough Sleep

You have to sleep for 7-8 hours. Many of you will laugh and argue that this suggestion is different. You may think you slept six hours as long as you could remember. Only on weekends, you sleep in. I will change your mind. I will change your mind.

You put your brain to rest while you sleep. You used your mind all day, and at night you need some sleep. Even if the mind never rests in the night (but that's another matter).

The mind is much more alert when you have enough sleep. The brain cells are healthy and will store information much more effectively and process information.

When you sleep enough, you feel relaxed and can focus much more on reality.

If we're tired, our level of concentration drops. Our ability to access information also decreases. When we're tired, it's much harder to remember. If drivers sleep on a seat, they are causing accidents. The explanation is that the brain wants to relax and cannot focus on the road.

You might be able to work and work with little sleep as normal, but it affects your memory.

3. Play Chess

Chess helps improve the consolidation of your memory. If you play chess, you focus on the game you are playing. You think of a few steps and try to think about a couple of tactics to win the game.

The more you concentrate and think, the more your brain works. It's a good brain workout.

One of the great benefits of chess is that it increases your focus because your mind doesn't wander. When we think normally, our mind will concentrate for a short time, and then you will get distracted by other issues.

It rarely happens when you play chess. You train the brain on how to concentrate, and this helps to maintain memory when you need it.

The maintenance of memory is successful if you plan by keeping the brain clean. The above tips help you to remain alert and memorize details if the opportunities are available.

If you want to take memory improvements seriously, you can read more information below. People who complain about memory loss problems usually try quick fixes but need to look after their brains in the long run.

CHAPTER 39

Power Up the Mind
Through Brain Training

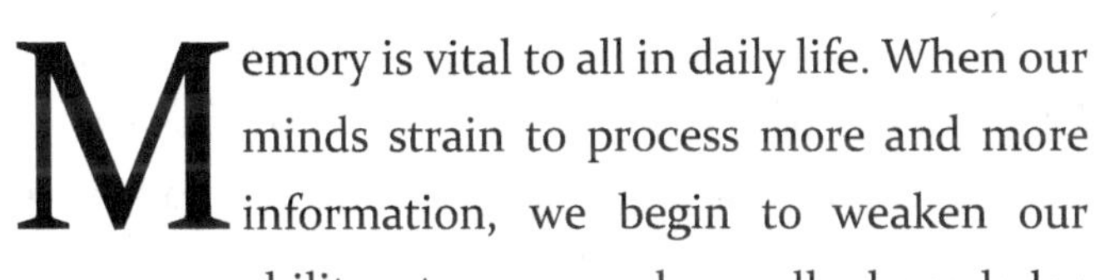

Memory is vital to all in daily life. When our minds strain to process more and more information, we begin to weaken our ability to remember all knowledge significantly. We mustn't forget. Forgetting even the simplest things can greatly influence us.

The good news is that we can all improve memory by studying strategies for memory restoration. Not only the left (technical) side of this technology but also the right (creative) side of the brain is used. Improving long-term memory helps to create a base on which to develop more nuanced and complex learning.

I have built myself the habit of repeating things. The more I practice, the better it got as my brain gets used to processing a lot of information each day. I keep a journal, too. By using a regular planner, I coordinate my life. Better organization can help free your concentrating powers so you can remember fewer routine things.

We have many tools to train our brains and increase our memory. Let me share with you a popular program in my country of origin, the Philippines. The software is known as Power Memory.

Power Memory is a groundbreaking learning system developed in 1999 by Ernie Aragon, a former University of the Philippines professor in microbiology. Power Memory equips people with superior memory skills to easily, effectively, systematically, and stress-free store, retain, and remember information. Among other methods, it uses imaginative interaction and imagination.

This curriculum focuses on the learner's attitudes. This covers people aged 8 to 80 years. Don't be afraid to try new things. Be sure because you know you have a good memory that will strengthen.

You will keep your brain healthy and enhance its physiological function through the development of new mental skills. If we have a good memory, our life will be more convenient!

New scientific work has shown that with the right mental preparation, we can improve the health and function of our brains. In a study funded by the National Health Institute, scientists found that brain training can improve memory, thinking, and processing speed. They found that mental gains lasted for at least five years!

CHAPTER 40

Easy Do's and Don'ts
Memory Improvement

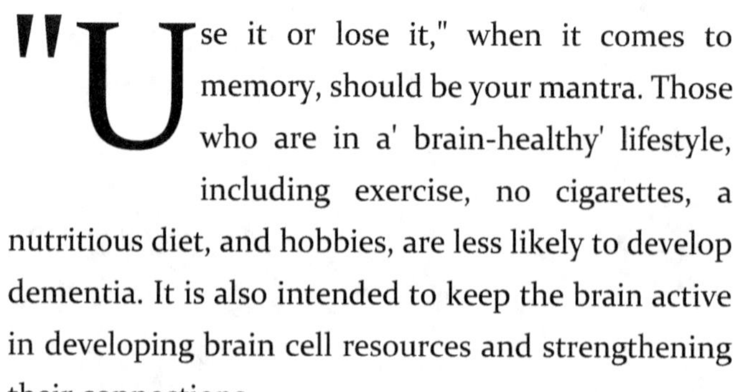

"Use it or lose it," when it comes to memory, should be your mantra. Those who are in a' brain-healthy' lifestyle, including exercise, no cigarettes, a nutritious diet, and hobbies, are less likely to develop dementia. It is also intended to keep the brain active in developing brain cell resources and strengthening their connections.

Things that are BAD for your MEMORY.

Under listed below is a list of things that will minimize our memory cycle.

Alcohol: messed with short-term memory and damaged brain dendrites that relay signals between brain cells. There are many different types of diseases caused by alcohol so that it is not heavily consumed.

Sleeplessness: May reduce your ability to recuperate memories and make you feel forgetful. It is very important to have plenty of sleep.

Smoking: Blocks blood circulation and oxygen into the brain. And many other smoking-related problems.

Stress: A new study has shown that stress stimulates an enzyme called kinase C that inhibits short-term memory. If you can't solve the problem, don't think about it. It doesn't do you any harm.

Other medicines: soothing agents, muscle relaxants, sleep pills, antidepressants, and high blood pressure drugs can sometimes help flirt or lead to some loss of memory. Be careful not to drive a car while taking drugs, too, since your reasoning is not very straightforward.

EAT FOR YOUR IQ Would you like to think smarter? Feed your mind, then.

Blueberries get their pigment from an antioxidant known as anthocyanin, which can improve their concentration, concentration, and short-term memory. Strawberries are known to have similar benefits and can protect them from loss of memory.

Broccoli Boost: This small crop is high in brain-working products, including medicine for Alzheimer's disease, by blocking an enzyme that induces the brain breakdown.

Good eggs: choline-high eggs, vitamin B-complexes. Lack of choline is related to impaired memory and concentration, while the correct amount will help brain cells communicate better.

Grain gains: Whole grains such as brown rice and rye bread filled with folate, B12, and B6 are used to break down chemicals such as homocysteine that are associated with Alzheimer's disease and heart disease at high levels.

Salmon Smart: cold-water fish are filled with a safe fatty acid called DHA (docosahexaenoic acid), including salmon, tuna, mackerel, and herring.

According to a new study at Stanford University in California, the brain only wants to recall memories that it feels are most important, ignoring those similar but less used, thereby increasing the cognitive load and preventing misunderstanding.

Don't be disappointed with the following memory tips if you keep forgetting something. This means that your brain works right. Nobody can remember it all. When you know what's important, that's what matters.

CHAPTER 41

Memory Improvement Tips for a Healthy Lifestyle

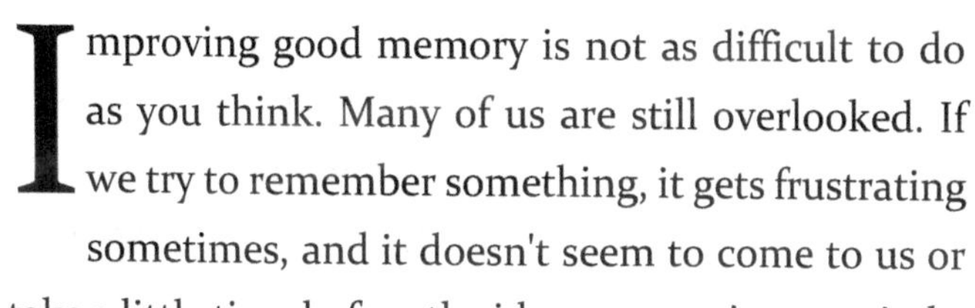

Improving good memory is not as difficult to do as you think. Many of us are still overlooked. If we try to remember something, it gets frustrating sometimes, and it doesn't seem to come to us or take a little time before the idea pops up in our minds.

While sometimes it's hard to deal with, it's not so often that we forget our memory, but that our minds are overcharged with too much thought at once.

There is good news if you are interested in ways to improve your memory. Your memory abilities are directly related to the health of your brain so that you can improve the health of your brain and recover the sharp memory of your youth. This is how...

Your ability to remember is, you would think, linked to the capacity of your brain to store and recall information. If your mind doesn't work properly or is faulty, your memory skills will suffer.

In reality, the brain works together with the five senses to make up learning and memory. Think of each of your five senses and their memories. The five senses of listening, feeling, seeing, smelling, and touching all lead to memory.

Let's remember, for starters, the sense of smell. You recall what it feels like being in the middle of an apple garden in fall. You will also remember the smell of your favorite pizza restaurant with baked pizza in brick furnaces. You can recall the familiar fresh scent of your car when you pulled off your last new vehicle.

Your brain works with your senses directly to store and retrieve information. But it needs to be fit and healthy if your brain is to function properly. There is no question that a highly functioning and balanced brain is the best way to improve memory.

Here are some tips to help keep your brain healthy: improving our memory isn't a problem, and it shouldn't be for anyone. Memorization can be hard most of the time, but you can improve it and maintain a good memory capacity.

I also suggest you learn some tips on improving your story and lifestyle. In my opinion, good health and a good memory are key to a successful life.

Understanding and knowing how our body and brain work can change the way we live our lives.

Like they say, "Knowledge is Power" and it's a must if you want to live a long time!

There are many ideas for better health and memory that we can talk about, but you should know the main ones.

For example, we need to eat fruit and vegetables every day or at least 5-6 days a week. Raspberries, Blueberries, Strawberries, Avocados, and Tomatoes are good for keeping the brain healthy.

A healthy mind will bring peace and positive energy to your life as you live and dream. Just take into account these memory changes and apply all that you know to your life, think about your health, and how beautiful life is, not to take care of it.

It's essential to eat fruits rich in antioxidants such as cranberries, as they keep them healthy. Also, in terms of improving performance, tuna, fish, salmon, and certain marine foods are very useful.

In adding fruit and vegetables to your diet, you are already taking a major step towards healthy living and good health. It's not difficult to make your diet. Try it! Try it!

The best tips for improving memory are those you find fun to do. Remember always to maintain a positive mindset, and you will meet the farthest goals.

Alright now, make sure you have fruit and vegetables every day or at least 4-5 days a week when you build your diet. Try to reduce junk food and unhealthy food. You won't hurt once in a while, but you will eventually learn how harmful this food can be for your body.

It is very important to eat proteins, so make sure that you consume your steak at least once a week. Or you can go to IHop and get yourself a T-Bone Steak with a cup of cold water and a salad on the side. If that makes it easier for you, it can work as well, but homemade food is typically better and healthier.

Writing

Writing and developing a healthy diet should be the first step towards a change in your life. It's a great step!

So take a notebook, pen, and dream of a diet, do not forget about fruits and veggies every day.

Keep or get alive through a healthy diet and exercise every day. You do not have to lift weights and run a marathon; just start walking a few days a day. Then try walking for a total of 5 days, 20 minutes a day.

Eat a Tomato. Eat a Flower.

Sure, fruits and vegetables also go a long way in a healthy body and a healthy mind. Drink plenty of water every day for your body. It's the biggest thing you can do.

You have to spend time out once in a while. You don't always have to be a great person. Avoiding pressure and letting your body and mind take a break from time to time will be of benefit to your brain.

Write down stuff. In writing things down, you can strengthen the mind. When you start to write a list, you only have to recall the list.

Stay Focused

You may have lots of information stored in your mind, but if you focus on one thing at a time, you will increase the chance of having more information.

Use Your Common Sense of God-Given Stuff.

Common sense is key when it comes to making decisions and maintaining your memory bank information. You've got seven senses. Use them all to help you understand what is happening in your busy life.

Join Your Day of Mind Games.

Card games, crossword puzzles, brainteasers, word association games, chess also keep your thoughts clear.

Change Your Attitude.

Your memory will fail if you have a poor attitude. Your mind will be a good world with a positive attitude. Consider visualizing to stimulate the mind and thought. I do it all the time, and it makes it much easier for me to remember!

Get the Right Amount of Sleep.

If you don't, you can't function correctly, and your mind will be nether. This is the best tip I can deliver. Have a good night's sleep, and in the morning, you will be going to a clearer mind.

Visualization

Visualization is always an important part of memory development. There are many more important facts relating to the human mind and the ability to remember things.

Add Dark Chocolate to Your Diet

Yes, what they're saying about dark chocolate is real. It's very good for you in moderation. Dark chocolate contains essential minerals that help make the brain dopamine. Dopamine is a drug that increases the brain's capacity and cognitive abilities. So go ahead, enjoy this rich treat of chocolate!

Improving Your Hearing Skills

An interesting way to enhance your listening skills is to choose a song you want and try to remember the messages. To do that, listen to the song as often as possible and write the lyrics in one place.

The actual practice of listening with a high concentration will, over time, develop your memory skills. You will be shocked how much better your memory is if you try one song a week.

Know (Or re-learn) a Musical Instrument

Allow it; you always wanted to play guitar, you wanted to? Mastering a musical instrument sharpens your mind by guiding your ears and converting the thoughts into sound. To play a new music piece,

You should read notes in a songbook and add the knowledge to the guitar strings with your hands.

Any method is created because it incorporates the same principles. It is not surprising why many musicians are renowned for their keen sense of remembrance.

Play Catch Yes, a Pass.

Play Catch If you don't have anybody to play with, throw a ball, and aim to catch it. Why? Why? Because it enhances the ability to coordinate and concentrate. These abilities affect the mind positively.

Seek to Juggle with Advanced Skills.

Like your body muscles, your brain must be a limb, versatile, and sensitive. Any practice contrary to your usual approach will help your brain process new information and boost your memory.

When you boost the brain's overall health, you will benefit greatly. Improving your brain health is one of the best techniques for improving your memory. You'll see a positive difference after these five tips for a couple of months. It's high time you develop an exercise routine and add it to your daily schedule. Training every day at least 10 to 15 minutes or at least three or four days per week is a great way to stay fit and keep your mind safe along with your healthy body.

This Monday, for example, you can take 10-20 jumping jackets, which will probably take no more than 3-4 minutes and can last for 5-10 minutes. Do this every morning; in a healthy and good mood, it will start your day. You can change it a little and do other activities.

I hope that these tips on memory recovery help you to improve your health. Please feel free to share your thoughts and ways of improving your health and memory, sometimes thinking about it helps you to realize what you are doing right or wrong.

CHAPTER 42

Tips to Improve Natural Memory

An incredible human brain contains around 100 billion neurons. Your brain receives about 100 million (different) messages per second with the ability to sort and transmit signals to other organs. Your brain can hold thousands of times more information than a computer.

It is the body's most unique, complex, and strong organ. The mind remains a mystery amid scientific inventions and discoveries. But the brain may experience certain disorders, the most common of which is memory loss. The section explains how you can develop your memory and concentration.

Some medical conditions lead to some memory problems; these conditions should be addressed before a complete solution to your memory loss can be found. Nevertheless, memory deficiency can be overcome by natural means in other circumstances. Here are some helpful tips for better memory.

Train your brain-the brain is made to work, like all other muscles; if you do not use it, you will lose it. Practice often to help him improve his performance.

Participate in matches that can improve the brain, chess, scrabble, etc. If possible. Many studies show that people who conduct advanced scientific experiments in their childhood are less at risk of developing amnesia.

Exercise-as in disease prevention, daily exercise is important to improve the functioning of your brain. To function properly, the body needs physical activities. Not only physical activity helps the brain's cells assimilate nutrients, but it also allows them to remove the accumulated contaminants in your brain.

Allow yourself social-Social isolation can decrease brain output-social exclusion can decrease brain performance. Consider yourself socially active, engage in activities, go with friends, try learning new things, read and meditate on the Bible, and so on. These things are powerful tools for better memory, although often overlooked.

Sleep well - it's now established after decades of debate that sleep plays a positive role in the consolidation of memory. A Harvard Medical School study showed a positive relationship between good sleep and the ability to stay focused. That's a better memory night. People who sleep regularly and undergo an examination perform much better.

Also, ventilate your home and office to encourage oxygenation of your brain cells, which improves your brain activity efficiency (studies and concentration) by 10 to 20 percent. Drink plenty of fluids, stop tobacco and alcohol, increasing concentration and vigilance.

A Healthy Diet

A healthy diet that includes foods rich in essential fatty acids like Omega 3 and DHA (a fatty acid that makes neurotransmitter release possible) is key. Additional supplements such as calcium, phosphorus, magnesium (found in milk, cheese, rice, vegetables, etc.) and complex B vitamins (found in wheat germ, brasser's yeast, yogurt, etc.) are required for active brain aid.

Your brain needs a range of substances to function effectively (vitamins, minerals, amino acids, essential fatty acids). A pure absence of these substances may induce a memory loss or imbalance.

The need to consume dietary supplements is, therefore, important for your brain to function properly. Nevertheless, it can be difficult to take these substances into a diet.

CONCLUSION

There are many ways to improve memory. All you need to do is periodically practice the strategies for memory improvement. The mind must be conditioned to maintain mental fitness.

When you can't remember your school's name and are upset with the loss of memory, exercise your brain with a few excellent strategies to memorize as much as possible. How quickly you can store and retrieve information shows how good your memory is. If it's not perfect, just like any other body function, you can change it easily.

Our brain serves as a storage device where all the required and unwanted information is stored as signals. Many people have an extremely sharp memory and can recall everything in no time, while others suffer from memory loss. Today there are many memory improving tools, strategies, and exercises that can help you significantly boost your memory.

Regular physical exercise or yoga is the perfect way to relax. It keeps you mentally and physically fit.

Research has shown that a person with a healthy body and a calm mind can remember things easily and have a strong memory.

People often lose their memory due to sleeplessness, anxiety, pressure, and depression. Yoga is one of the best ways to release stress and anxiety and allow you to sleep better. When you consistently begin to practice, you will find a marked change in your ability to retain and remember things.

Mind exercise is a completely different kind of exercise that does not have anything to do with physical exercise. Simple mathematics is an effective way to improve memory.

Different games and puzzles offer great ways to train your mind. Get a book of puzzles and solve some puzzles or questions every day and enjoy the memory difference.

You can also boost your memory when you concentrate on the specifics and recall them in the same order. You must have found that most in serial order, you cannot recall anything.

Taking a few moments to achieve a simple memory change and write something in some sequence. Just concentrate on remembering and trying to remember it in 8-10 seconds. You may not be able to execute this completely at first, but you will eventually succeed in it.

Our sleep system has an important role to play. A night of deep sleep is important not just for our health and fine body but also for our mental well-being. If it is disrupted, try to improve the sleep-waking schedule.

The technique of connection building is very helpful in the collection of information. It does not improve your memory, nor helps you to remember names, numbers consciously. Build some amusing ties around the names of your friend, phone numbers, license number, bank account number, etc.

Whenever you need to use them, you won't have problems remembering them. This is by no means a memory improvement or improvement technique, and rather it allows you to recall the information.